OSCAR & LUCY

An Autobiographical Biography

Alan Kennedy

LASSERRADE

ALAN KENNEDY AND THE PROF, MELBOURNE, 1964

Copyright © Alan Kennedy 2014

ISBN 978-0-9564696-8-7

Alan Kennedy has asserted his right under the Copyright Designs and Patents Act 1988 to be identified as the author of this work

First published in the United Kingdom in 2014 by Lasserrade Press

For EWK

Introduction

This is not an orthodox biography; neither is it really much of an autobiography; also, it is not about anybody called Lucy: it is something between all three of these things. The book came into being by accident. I was wrestling with my novel *Lucy*, finding myself, as ever, fighting a character. And for reasons that lie too deep for thought I found myself musing about my father's days in wartime England. Which led me inexorably to Oscar, my old Professor in Melbourne years and years ago. Why was that? I was left amazed afresh at the subtlety of the process we call reminding; at its intricacy; at its ability to surprise the very mind that is working the magic. How close are recovered memories to fiction? Certainly, my Melbourne days were so long ago their story might well belong to another person. Was that terror-stricken young lecturer trying to come to terms with his first academic Big Fish really me? I look back at him and realise he is hardly to be distinguished from a fiction. So you can say it was psychological curiosity that brought me here. I know (or think I know) the forces that shaped my life; the forces that carried me here more or less in one piece. What were the forces that shaped Oscar? Is it possible to know?

Oscar was one of those people blessed (or is it cursed?) to live in interesting times; indeed, times interesting enough for a dozen normal lives. He was the architect of extraordinary – even heroic - deeds, yet they are completely forgotten now. He was to be counted along with people who shaped the history of the 20th Century, but he is barely mentioned. He was a psychologist who worked with giants, someone who made crucial discoveries in psychology, yet came to distrust the discipline and finally almost to disown it. The history of Oscar's move from brilliant physics graduate to disillusioned professor perfectly illustrates fault lines in our infant discipline of psychology: fault lines that have remained for a century or more.

Because this is also a book about the problems of psychology – a subject to which, like Oscar, I have devoted the best part of my life. My quest was a little like Oscar's – I think both of us were looking for a kind of psychology that was, in some way, *authentic*; a psychology not forever doomed to a metaphorical existence. All students are taught that scientific psychology was born in 1879 - in Wundt's laboratory in Leipzig. The fact that word "laboratory" rings a little false is not accidental. A moment's reflection suggests that Leipzig could only have been the cradle of psychology in a very restricted sense. For example, Jean-Martin Charcot, the neurologist who introduced the young Freud to hypnotism, had been studying a variety of psychological disorders in Paris for many years before then. And eminent men of science, like Charles Wheatstone and David Brewster in England, had been studying stereoscopic vision since the 1830s. The history of "psychology" plainly reaches back to antiquity – at least as far as Plato's reflections on ideal forms. Nonetheless, the contribution of the spade-bearded Wilhelm Wundt was truly distinctive; it touches on an intellectual puzzle that will echo through the rest of this book. Trained as a physiologist and a philosopher, he tried to detach the study of the mind from both disciplines. Can you describe conscious experience as something other than a physiological process – a curiosity built out of nerve cells? Is there more than metaphysics to be done with human mentation? If a genuinely authentic psychology is to exist it must be neither a branch of physiology nor philosophy. That was Wundt's ambition.

He failed. Indeed, nearly a hundred and fifty years on psychology's fate remains just as uncertain. On one side of the fork, much of contemporary psychology has no independent life at all - it has been subsumed by neurology. Thought is now seen as a correlate of neural activity in the brain. But if you wonder what it would mean to have a neural account of *sensation* most psychologists look away – the question is embarrassing. The other arm of this fork has proved equally unsatisfactory. Philosophy now barely concerns itself with metaphysics: revelling in a kind of pessimistic nihilism, it has pretty well given up on science altogether. There are better ways of construing the world, we are told, than bothering with the mechanistic preoccupations of the nineteenth century. The consequences of this for psychology have been spectacular and disastrous, unleashing a post-modern revolution in which empirical observation (what we used to call facts) has become literally impossible. Certainly psychology can speak, but it must now do so with a multitude of competing voices. Authority rests largely on political allegiance; it has become a matter of opinion.

All these years after Wundt, psychology can still only offer "as if" explanations. We remain practitioners of a largely metaphorical discipline. Oscar lived long enough to see the rise and fall of many metaphors for human mental life including - rather absurdly – animal models. He also lived through a time of unparalleled turmoil in which the aftermath of two world wars presented psychologists with urgent practical problems. As you will discover, in some ways we didn't fare too badly. In others, the achievements are more difficult to assess.

I sense you losing heart already. You think I am about to dredge up the mildly diverting deeds of some long-forgotten fogey. I know what you mean – that would be a dispiriting affair. But you would be wrong. Do not doubt me on the subject of Oscar - he really was an extraordinary man and the extraordinary times through which he lived were in no small measure shaped by what he did. Read on.

It was a creeping sort of place, Dundee, filled with war-weary people. Barely a city, just a muddle of tiny houses with sour gardens, bleak stone tenements their fronts blackened with smoke, narrow twisted streets, sullen pends petering out to nothing, paved closes spattered by the drips from washing trailing high above. All ringed by the gaunt bricks of towering mills. Mills everywhere, shaking the pavements, an endless underlying throb to daily life. Dundee was a city of widows, inured to death, half its men gone years ago, whole regiments lost in the mud of the Western Front, bodies past counting. A city of half-men, the ones left over, blind or maimed, the lucky ones, no longer fit for the mill. What can you paint in a city of dead people?

Lucy, 2014

CHAPTER 1

The war baby

My dad was not in the war - that's to say, the Second World War. He tended to steer the conversation away when the subject came up. At least, that was what I assumed he was doing. I was very young, but I assumed he was ashamed, and that belief rather coloured my view of the old man. After all, my chums at school all had dads who had helped conquer the Third Reich: they had been builders of fantastic escape gliders, diggers of tunnels, architects of impossibly daring impersonations. You remember the hero in *Rogue Male*? I assure you he was modelled on the dads of my chums at school, every one of them.

After a while, we three boys got out of the way of asking dad about the war. Of course, we asked his brother because he had been in the navy. Being very little I managed to confuse this with his being a pirate – something to do with ships, anyway. Uncle Arthur kept three little boys spellbound with stories of the Atlantic convoys, little knowing that at least one of them had him standing on the poop deck under billowing sails, a telescope to his eye. The eye without the patch, that is. And there was Uncle Ken as well, modest pacific Uncle Ken, who would, if you got him in the right mood, sitting down with his whisky, go on at length about the drive towards Tripoli. He was almost as vague as we were as to the exact location of Tripoli, but it seemed an exciting sort of place, full of sand. Perhaps a little like Teignmouth.

There's no doubt about it, dad came off quite badly in all this. He seemed to have escaped the war without deserving to. Without even digging a tunnel or strangling a guard (I had a friend at school who showed me how to strangle a guard – he had been entrusted with this secret by his father). Dad had escaped by the simple device of not being there in the first place, and that would never do. Being ashamed – he must have been ashamed – insidiously infected his three boys. We stopped asking and he stopped avoiding: it became white space on the family page.

Plays on the wireless when I was a boy rarely missed the chance to use the "air raid warning" siren as a sound effect. You still hear it now and again - a melancholy wail rising slowly out of nothing then hanging on far too long, like somebody holding their breath. I suppose it was meant to reassure – it was, after all, a sort of confirmation for those listening that this was not for real. But Mother hated the sound; she couldn't bear it. A hatred out of all proportion. The psychologist in me now would say an unreasoning pathological hatred. Except I wasn't a psychologist then and for years I never even asked myself why she couldn't bear the way that sound went on and on: why she hated that it didn't stop. She would rush from the room, covering her ears, or, if she had the cat on her knee, grip the arms of the chair and speak far too quietly for her own good. So quietly it frightened us. "Turn it off, Bob," she would say. And he always did.

Did I think less of him because of this awful cowardice? Did knowing he was a coward enter my infant mind? Certainly a coward was one thing you couldn't be at my school and the masters clearly suspected it was a heritable trait. These were hard-bitten disillusioned men, some of whom hung on to their titles – Major this or Captain that. Men who'd finished their war and ended up, for want of anything better, drumming French into little boys. So, quite early on, I came to fear that dad had been a secret conshie. One boy's father had been an acknowledged conshie. He did his best to fake being proud of it but he was a scuttling cowardly sort of boy, witness to his unspeakable father, the conshie. Whatever that was – we were never very clear. But the masters knew; particularly, they knew. So perhaps I did think less of dad, and in truth we never got on at all well. Not on account of his failure - even the vicar explained we must forgive that. But for the effect his failure had on me, or at least might have had. Undeserved second-hand opprobrium: what could be worse than that?

Which makes it difficult for me even to write these words. I got the old man wrong – completely wrong.

Looking back, I see that my father had the worst of two worlds. Not called up because his occupation was "reserved", he lived feeling guilty about a distant abstract war while a real war, all too close, dogged his every day and drove my mother mad. He was drafted (or volunteered, it is a distinction he didn't make) to join a relatively suicidal team of electrical engineers in charge of the power station inside a huge ICI factory. His job was to keep the lights blazing in a little part of blackout England. The letters stood for Imperial Chemical Industries, a vast conglomerate; owners, among many other things, of Nobel Explosives. This well-lit factory was filled with high explosive.

Now and then dad would work a night shift, setting off every evening at about seven, with meticulously prepared marmalade sandwiches wrapped in grease-proof paper, and a packet of Players. To keep the lights burning in a place that manufactured explosives. Not only explosives; the factory also made sulphuric and nitric acid and the chemicals used to "make smoke" at sea. Unsurprisingly, this well-illuminated sitting target was bombed pretty well every week. Mostly the bombs missed, because the defences discouraged flying at low altitude. Nonetheless, every now and then some outpost or other would disappear. Simply vanish, vaporised in a quick fireball, together with the occupants. They were the ones who didn't go home next morning. In fact, they didn't go anywhere: they were so completely gone there wasn't even anything left to bury. Much of my mother's war was spent wondering whether she would ever see again the man she'd made the marmalade sandwiches for. The waiting sent her mad: she never recovered.

Bit by bit, years later, the true story of my father's war seeped into the lives of we three brothers. It was far too late for him to be a hero. Perhaps he should have explained. Perhaps he assumed we knew all the time. Perhaps he forgave us for forgiving him – I'll never know.

CHAPTER 2

Trying to telling the truth

THE psychologist Kenneth Pope has an interesting description of a meeting in the early years of the American Psychological Association; a significant meeting that became part of psychological folklore. It has never been very clear *where* it took place, but the *when* is more certain: July 1892 - July the eighth to be precise. Some of the giants of the discipline were there, people like William James, James Cattell and Joseph Jastrow. Pope goes on to explain that forty odd years later, someone was commissioned to write a history of the Association and reached the point where he had to describe this famous meeting. He realised that two of those present (Cattell and Jastrow) were actually still alive, so he asked them what went on, what was discussed and so forth. After all, a little circumstantial detail can go a long way to brighten up a dull history. Both men denied ever having been at such a meeting. Indeed, they were so convincing in their denial that it became clear it never took place. The memory of the event – in this case an oft-repeated shared memory – was quite simply false.

I want to consider the mental activity we call reminding. How did Proust's madeleine biscuit have that magical effect? How did thinking about my father and his miserable war come to remind me of Oscar? Because it certainly did. You may well ask, Who's Oscar anyway? but you'll have to be patient on that score – we have work to do first and I have to say more than a little about the psychology of memory.

When I started out on the rutted road to a career as a professional psychologist I chose to write a doctoral thesis on why we forget. If I had been wiser I would have asked why we remember, for that is surely the more interesting question. But I was young and, after all, forgetting is interesting enough. Shakespeare (at least in the early plays) offers two accounts of memory failure. The first notion is that new memories replace old ones. He's a bit vague as to where the old ones go: you're left assuming they simply vanish. The second idea rests on the ancient belief that memories are like impressions on a wax tablet. Hence, although the message may be potent, the medium isn't, and memories disappear because what supports them wears out.

My own modest research confirmed a conclusion that was already well known. Memory could not possibly work along either of the lines sketched out by Shakespeare. The truth was altogether more bizarre – even a little frightening – but to appreciate that you have to go back a bit.

In 1899, not long after the meeting that never took place, Sigmund Freud wrote a brief account of the memories of one of his patients. It was an essay on what he called Screen Memory: the patient under psychoanalysis uses an early memory – in this case charged with sexual symbolism - to screen his later memory of an adolescent love affair (in other words, the precise reverse of Shakespeare's first idea.)

This is what the patient reported:

> *I see a rectangular, rather steeply sloping piece of meadow-land, green and thickly grown; in the green there are a great number of yellow flowers -- evidently common dandelions. At the top end of the meadow there is a cottage, and in front of the cottage door two women are chatting busily, a peasant woman with a handkerchief on her head and a children's nurse. Three children are playing in the grass. One of them is myself (between the age of two and three); the two others are my boy cousin, who is a year older than me, and his sister, who is almost exactly the same age as I am. We*

> *are picking the yellow flowers and each of us is holding a bunch of flowers we have already picked. The little girl has the best bunch; and as though by mutual agreement, we -- the two boys -- fall on her and snatch away her flowers. She runs up the meadow in tears and as a consolation the peasant-woman gives her a big piece of black bread. Hardly have we seen this than we throw the flowers away, hurry to the cottage, and ask to be given some bread too. And we are in fact given some; the peasant-woman cuts the loaf with a long knife. In my memory the bread tastes quite delicious -- and at that point the scene breaks off.*

To the right professional eyes this catalogue of sexual symbolism is almost comically explicit, squeezing in bed-wetting, masturbation, rape and castration along with the yellow flowers (I know the links are a bit obscure, but then so is psychoanalysis, believe me). It's tempting, but I'm not going to discuss all that; I will simply point to what the patient went on to say, and that's not obscure at all:

> *It seems to me almost a certainty that this childhood memory never occurred to me at all in my earlier years.*

Freud's conclusion on the subject was equally radical:

> *It may indeed be questioned whether we have any memories at all from our childhood: memories relating to our childhood may be all that we possess. Our childhood memories show us our earliest years not as they were but as they appeared at the later periods when the memories were aroused. In these periods of arousal, the childhood memories did not, as people are accustomed to say, emerge; they were formed at that time. And a number of motives, with no concern for historical accuracy, had a part in forming them, as well as in the selection of the memories themselves.*

The idea that memory is a matter of active construction ("with no concern for historical accuracy") rather than passive recovery was taken up and developed in Sir Frederick Bartlett's book *Remembering*, published in 1932 (remember that date, if you would, it will come in useful later). Bartlett was professor of psychology at Cambridge University – a very remarkable man who will loom large in this tale.

Rather than look at specific memories and dreams, Bartlett carried out deceptively simple experiments in which people read folk stories and then, much later, were probed to see how well they remembered what they had read. They didn't do too badly, all things considered. But the results were far more interesting than that. Memories were distorted in systematic ways: assimilated into the beliefs and attitudes of the readers. Much of what was remembered was plausible and coherent, and could well have been something previously read. But it was false; invented; made up. People were sure of what they remembered, and it made sense to them. Indeed, often it made more sense than the original. The problem was, it bore little relation to what they had read.

This is starting to sound quite alarming. Is memory that malleable? that unreliable? We spend a lot of our time interacting with other people, talking to them, laughing with them. We remember things about them, what they have said to us in the past, what we have said to them. When I am talking to you I believe your memories of what I said to you the other day are the same as mine. What if I'm wrong? William James (one of those at the meeting that didn't take place) was the brother of Henry James, the author. In writing about memory he (that is, William) tellingly compared it to fiction. Fiction, he said, has this unique ability to expel reality from memory and "reign in its stead alone". In that regard we are all authors: we are authors of ourselves. The personal history that defines and sustains us, the rehearsed fragments of life we cherish or fear - encounters, kisses, trials, humiliations, battles – is an intricate world of fictions. Fictions that long ago displaced reality, if indeed there ever was a reality. Memories are, consequently, quite often false. Oddly enough, they may true to something else, albeit false to the facts – we shall come to that later. The ability to believe contradictory things is what makes us human. The fact that we routinely accept mutually inconsistent chains of inference allows us to function as social (or political) animals. Incidentally, it also allows writers of detective fiction to earn an honest crust.

Although Bartlett's studies were interesting and thought-provoking they were, after all, only psychological experiments. Surely memory in reality – in what we tend to call the real world – is more stable, more reliable? After all, we rely on it in the legal process. What lawyers and policemen call evidence often boils down to what somebody remembers. Surely if you do your best to tell the truth, the whole truth and nothing but the truth? Surely, if you add, "So help me God" – as some are wont to do – the truth will emerge? Well, truth's a tricky thing: Pilate, you may recall, asked about it at the trial of Jesus, and then didn't hang around for an answer.

As luck would have it, in 1972 a trial far less significant than that of Jesus gave psychologists the opportunity they had been waiting for to examine the question in detail. I am referring to the doings of the famous committee of the US Senate set up to look into the burglary at the Watergate Centre and the subsequent cover-up of that event by White House staff. President Nixon had been re-elected, but the belief that he had been personally implicated in this skulduggery would not go away. The Watergate Hearings effectively sealed his fate. Bit by bit, the testimony of those present, their memories of meetings and conversations, formed itself into a coherent picture. Slowly, Tricky Dicky's goose was cooked.

The key witness in this affair was a man called John Dean, the former counsel to the President. His evidence was a chronicle of encounters with Nixon stretching back over many years. In particular, what Dean remembered of conversations involving John Mitchell and Robert Haldeman helped bring a President down. Dean's memory was phenomenal. Senators commented on the clarity and consistency of his recall. He was even jokingly referred to as a human tape recorder. Which became hardly a joke at all when, not long afterwards, it emerged that those meetings and conversations had, in fact, been secretly recorded. All of them. By the President himself.

With Nixon's reputation in tatters and with the office of President mired in disgrace, the news that these tapes existed was greeted with a mixture of disbelief and bemusement. Obviously, prosecutors wanted them. Obviously, after due process, prosecutors would get them. Commentators publicly speculated on the former President's vanity. It seemed foolhardy to the point of madness to have kept such damaging testimony. Why on earth hadn't the guy destroyed them when he had the chance? Yet oddly enough it was the President himself who arranged for publication of the transcripts. He even wrote a foreword which amounted to the claim that Dean's memory of events had been entirely false.

For people in my profession it fell to the cognitive psychologist Ulric Neisser to carry out the necessary analysis, finally published in 1981 as "John Dean's Memory: a Case Study" – a classic of cognitive psychology. Like all clever ideas it was obvious when you thought about it: take a particular event and compare Dean's memory for what was said with what actually was said. It is something that can be done word by word – a curiously eerie operation, because it is so rare.

Well, what did Neisser discover? Dean's fabled memory for detail was simply that – a fable. He was virtually always wrong about detail. Crucially, he was wrong on legally significant points of detail that Senators had pursued: whether the President himself had actually uttered particular words or merely allowed them to be said in his presence. You can see why Nixon felt that the record would vindicate him: he never did (quite) say any of the things Dean alleged. Dean's memory was wrong. Worse than that, his memory was equally bad when you came to the gist of things said and done. More often than not he distorted the gist of a conversation, exaggerating his own role and sometimes even inventing a role for himself where none existed. In a nutshell, you could not use Dean's memory of events to recover anything like the truth of what went on. At pretty well all levels, what he remembered was quite manifestly false. People didn't say what he recalled them saying; people didn't do what he said they did; and so on.

So was Dean a liar? So was the President innocent after all? Fortunately, this is a chapter about memory so I will finesse those questions. Dean was no more a liar than anybody else. And that includes me (and you). He believed he was telling the truth. Alas, he also believed, as do I (and you), that he had preserved a record of the past, when all he had preserved was a record of *his* past. As Freud might have put it, John Dean's testimony related to John Dean. His memories didn't emerge like a stack of file cards, they were formed, to use Freud's term, by the circumstance of the Watergate Hearings. Circumstances that included the fact that he believed, along with most people, that President Nixon was guilty. According to Neisser, Dean was "fundamentally right" about what had happened, despite the fact that his testimony was (almost invariably) wrong. Imagine you are in the jury at a trial. The Judge sums up: "Nothing the key witness said has proved to be correct, and we have irrefutable evidence of that, ladies and gentlemen of the jury. Nothing he said can be substantiated by reference to that record. Indeed, the defence has described it as a pack of lies, and it is hard to quarrel with that. Nothing he said was true … nothing save his manifest and sincere belief in the guilt of the prisoner …" Would you feel a little awkward? Would you wriggle slightly? Which does rather put the spotlight on Ulric Neisser.

Having demonstrated that Dean told the truth about virtually nothing, it is interesting to see how Neisser squares this with the claim he was "accurate" as to the fact of Nixon's complicity in a crime. He poses the question in a disarming way: "Given the numerous errors in his reports of conversations, what did he tell the truth about?" I must say, the answer is a bit strange. We are told John Dean did not misrepresent the truth (that Nixon was guilty) because in the course of numerous encounters with the President he had formed a clear view as to his complicity. He didn't misrepresent this knowledge, he just "dramatized" it, using narrative processes which are, as we have seen, the very stuff of memory. In that respect, he was consistent, even accurate. We are to believe his consistency reflected a deeper truth, independent of the particularities of detail. Stripped of the fancy words, what Neisser is saying is that Dean told a good story: a story that grew out of innumerable encounters with a seriously delinquent President; a story that resonated because we too knew it to be true (I'll hurry past that last point). So the President's hopes that Dean's testimony would be undermined because it was wrong in both gist and detail (virtually all its details, mind you) were doomed, because at another level – for want of a better term, what we might call the level of God's truth - what Dean had said was accurate. Neisser ends his paper saying this about Dean: "His mind was not a tape recorder, but it certainly received the message that was being given."

I don't know about you, but I find that conclusion quite scary. I'm not lighting any candles for Richard Nixon, you understand, but I find the idea of what I might call "justified falsehood" rather disturbing. Because it is barely a step away from the unjustified kind. Indeed, because it can lead to all kinds of perverse consequences. I fully accept that personal memories are creations, personal fictions making up the sustaining web of my identity. Equally, I can accept that shared memories are often negotiated fictions – the stories we tell each other, the stories we mutually inhabit. I can accept that the difference between memory and belief hardly bears scrutiny and dissolves on inspection. All this I can accept. But I worry nonetheless. I worry about certainty. I worry about conviction. I worry that one can still ask the question, "What is truth?"

You may judge I'm getting to the point at long last. But first let me remind you I am telling a story and a story must make sense.

This particular story will make *my* sense – not necessarily yours. And since it will be as much about me as about Oscar I run the same risks as John Dean: just bear it in mind. Well, am I going to explain exactly how Proust's madeleine cake had that extraordinary effect? Am I going to tell you about Oscar? Soon, soon, I promise, but let me tell you another story first. Twenty years ago or more I was in a queue at a conference lunch break. Inching my way along with my tray, the way you do at these things. I was late and there was nothing much I fancied apart from some nice looking pieces of battered fish. Only a few pieces were left; it's always that way. Indeed, by the time I was within range there were only two pieces left in the tray. The man in front (I confess a rival of mine) took one, hesitated, glanced briefly down at my shoes in a shifty sort of way, and then took the last piece as well. Sounds familiar? I suppose so. Now don't you go believing the circumstantial detail – not after everything I've said. But at least accept that the Battle of the Fish took place. I ruminate on it often - I suppose because I lost. Now, speed forward to just the other day, I pulled into an underground car park. It was completely full. I made the usual myopic circuit in the semi-dark and was about to leave when a car started to inch out of its bay. The way they do, the tell-tail exhaust steaming in an encouraging fashion. I stopped, waiting to take the place, only too aware of blocking those behind me. My waiting form was observed and the moving car crept slowly back into its bay. And there it stayed, immobile, while the occupant lit a cigarette. And suddenly, like Proust, I was a thousand miles away, inching my way towards those last bits of fish.

CHAPTER 3

Enter The Prof

To describe my early years as a psychologist I have to invoke that term beloved of P G Wodehouse fans, "unseen forces were at work". You'll see why in a minute. Possessed of a PhD, based on a thesis written rapidly to avoid starvation, I knew a good bit about memory. Or to be strictly truthful I knew a great deal more about forgetting. I was on excellent terms with my benevolent supervisor (his first name was Harry). He had spent happy days in the immediate post-war years in Australia at Melbourne University, combining teaching psychology with raising sheep (yes, the parallel struck me as well). Harry spoke feelingly about that egalitarian paradise, where every citizen could have their time at "The Uni". It would bring tears to his eyes. The idea of mass education seemed extraordinarily exciting to me at that time - probably because I was young and had not thought about it very much. The prospect of the whole world sharing my enthusiasm for Retroactive Inhibition (you'll have to look it up) seemed exciting beyond belief. One afternoon, over a cup of tea, I was rash enough to share this enthusiasm with Harry. He took it as evidence of my long-awaited political awakening and the conversation ended with his rubbing his hands together and saying, I'll see whether I can get you a job there - you'll like it. He was on the way out of the room, but I'm pretty sure that's what he said.

Thus it came about that some four hectic months later, my new wife and I were planning to emigrate to Australia. Believe it or not, you could do this for ten quid each, on condition that you didn't come back. Initially allocated a berth on an Italian liner, my case was upgraded to air travel because (I refer you to the paragraph above) *I had a job to go to*. The italic is to illustrate how this phrase became a leitmotif in my cloistered life at that time. Now you are probably imagining lengthy negotiations with my future employer. You imagine the frustration of air mail exchanges in days before email, indeed at a time when possessing a domestic computer would have seemed a ridiculous fancy. You're thinking perhaps that lawyers were involved, eagerly striking out phrases, inserting codicils or whatever they do, until a contract could resolutely be signed. Such is the power of recollection, you may even remember the pen involved – perhaps it was my Parker with the gold nib. Of course, you would be quite wrong. Certainly, life at that time was consumed with the practicalities of shipping new wife and myself to the other side of the world; together with all we possessed (not a great deal, by the way). But the actual job when I got there concerned me hardly at all. After all, I could call myself "Dr" now. And Harry had received a letter one day from somebody he called "The Prof." I didn't actually possess a copy of this letter, photocopiers not having been invented, but Harry had read out the critical bit one morning over a cup of tea. You will have read the previous chapter, so *caveat emptor*, but from memory the bit in the letter went something like: Yes, this chap sounds interesting. We've been thinking of building up our experimental side. I should think we can find him something. There are always tutor jobs going. That's the gist of it. It was very nice to be thought interesting - I was almost tempted to take up smoking.

Before you run away with the idea I was being a bit naive, I should point out that Harry took it on himself to offer an extended exegesis on his letter and its true import. He explained that this was how the academic dog wagged its tail. Letters are written pointing out the merits of this or that favoured protégé until eventually they find their place. It seemed a bit haphazard to me but, as I mentioned, I was young at the time. In any case, I warmed to this Prof chap, in as much as he had been perceptive enough to see my merits and find me interesting on so little evidence. Briefly, I was not so much wet behind the ears as wet all over - the result of passing through life to that point with the sole objective of keeping up with the scholarly literature on memory and not much else. Really, virtually nothing. Indeed, it is an enduring mystery to me how I had managed to acquire a wife. And if you have difficulty imagining this innocent cast into a cruel and uncaring world and wonder how he could possibly have survived, it is a difficulty I share. An appeal to unseen forces is the best I can offer for the time being.

So the passage was booked and at all suitable times (they were many, believe me, this being something of an Australian obsession) the mantra *I have a job to go to* was repeated.

And thus it came to pass I met The Prof.

My somewhat put-upon wife and I arrived in Flinders Street Railway Station - an imposing affair in downtown Melbourne - early one morning in a January heatwave. Later that afternoon I took a tram ride to the equally imposing Psychology Department and reported for work. I didn't actually expect to begin that very day, you understand: that would have been naive. I imagined certain formalities; perhaps a form or two to be filled in. As luck would have it, that day The Prof was in. Up to that time I had had limited experience of elevated academics. Those I knew were nearly always "in" - reading or drinking tea, or combining the two activities. Harry, for example, was so much always in that I never knew him to be anywhere else. Apparently it was not so with The Prof.

Having extracted my name (an early opportunity to brandish my "Dr") and my address, I was told I was lucky, the means of this telling being so severe a little unease entered my breast. I stood awkwardly in the vast outer office suddenly imagining I had been written into the second reel of one of those Hollywood movies where the ingenuous danseuse, armed only with her innocence and her long legs accidentally walks right into the office of the biggest agent in town (the one nobody ever sees –

the one with the cigar). It was a bit like that, although without the legs. After an interminable wait I was ushered in by the dragon secretary and stood before the great man. I can only assume The Prof had little on that afternoon and the notion of seeing me clearly had comic possibilities given the story I had told the dragon.

We got off to a halting start, The Prof and I, because he could not remember writing to Harry. Indeed, his questions were clearly designed to determine who exactly Harry was. He managed a slight frown suggesting if he worked at it, the name might come to him. It was only when I raised the matter of my imminent employment that little silences started to fall into our exchanges. Some of these were quite long. There appeared to be what psycholinguists term a conflict of presuppositions. However you wrap it up, it's best that presuppositions should not clash when its a matter of having a job. Or, in my case, not having one. I confess my recollection of the rest of that meeting is hazy. The conversation morphed into a discussion of memory and went on for some time. I recall mentioning interesting research on severe trauma and anterograde memory loss. I sat down at that point to avoid making it seem too personal, but work on memory and shell shock would keep worming its way in. I'm afraid the details are gone. Only the emotional tone is preserved. I would characterise this as anxiety, except hysterical panic seems more apposite. Not nice anyway, and it would do me a favour if it went the same way as the details. But alas, there are some things you can't forget. Not that the fault lay with The Prof, you understand. That's rather the point.

That evening in our rented rooms I explained three things to my wife. I can't swear to the order but they covered the fact that Harry had possibly exaggerated his job-fixing abilities, that The Prof was rather a formidable character, and that I didn't appear to have any immediate prospects of gainful employment. She had spent the afternoon dealing with an antipodean spider of such prodigious size she had initially taken it to be a discarded toy. Until it walked up the wall, that is. It was one of those days. Frankly, I felt like having a really good cry.

Two days later I got a short letter from somebody I eventually worked out must have been the dragon herself. It was bulky because there was a lengthy contract of employment enclosed, in duplicate. Subject only to my providing proof of my PhD, I was offered a job. The letter pointed out that the three unpaid weeks before the job started could usefully be spent familiarising myself with the Department. The key to my room could be collected during office hours from The Technical Services Officer. I was not invited to visit The Prof. Indeed, there was no indication he had interested himself in the matter.

Now you may think things in the real world don't evolve like this; that there must be a back story; that it's all a bit peculiar. But they do; and there is; and you're right. For the moment think of unseen forces. For myself, had I been better read, I would have been thinking about angels. But I thought of no such thing. I dutifully filled in my three unpaid weeks, found my PhD Certificate, and began work as a Senior Tutor in Psychology in the University of Melbourne. My first academic job.

The Prof's name was Oscar.

CHAPTER 4

The academic galley slave

He turned out to be a bit strange, The Prof. For one thing, he was virtually invisible: I never saw him. Yet I knew when he was there because this coincided with unusual ferocity in his guarding dragon. I entertained two hypotheses about this situation. Possibly he sneaked into the place incredibly early. But I was forced to do that (see below) and I saw neither hair nor hide of him, however early I arrived. Possibly he actually lived in his office, sleeping there. This seemed implausible. It remained a mystery and slowly this absent presence became not so much strange as scary. I should add, I was easily scared.

You recall that visit concerning my first job? What you might entitle "Harry's Bequest" if you were writing fiction. On that day The Prof had been in and I had seen him. As his weeks of invisibility stretched into months I came to realise what a rare and wonderful accident this had been. I told you there were angels.

The Prof manifested himself to humble tutors in writing. Limp sheets of damp paper printed in blurred purple ink and smelling of alcohol. The kind used by doctors to wipe your arm before an injection. I hated injections at that time, so virtually every day my pulse was set racing on account of those damned missives. It was humiliating to have my heart regulated by the letter box, but there you are, Pavlov decreed it would be so and I was in a Psychology Department, after all: places where you learn that explaining behaviour doesn't mean you can change it. These memoranda were the product of an impressive duplicating system, a kind of massive automated John Bull Printing Kit, comprising a hand operated drum, a pad soaked in a dangerously volatile liquid, and suitably absorbent paper. High end technology, and for the exclusive use of The Prof.

The actual messages managed to combine the gnomic with the laconic – an art form yet to find its proper place. You might come in to discover in your letter box, "I look in vain for evidence that last Monday was a Bank Holiday". Once, I received, "I remind colleagues that the word 'data' is plural." Wounding, because I shared The Prof's sensitivity on that point. You note the hint of asperity and the signature use of the present tense? On days when you got a flurry of these things you started to believe your life had been scripted by Damon Runyon. The Prof also did his bit in purple to save the apostrophe, a cause lost even then. But your heart warms to him for trying - well, mine did. Was it worth all that alcohol? A deep question, dear reader, best saved for the long winter evenings.

You recall I was to begin my academic life as a tutor under the watchful eye of The Prof. How he actually did this watching I never discovered, but I was unnervingly conscious of it nonetheless. I was a Senior Tutor because I was a Dr. But don't be fooled by that "Senior" stuff – tutors, whether senior or not, were psychological galley slaves. True, we didn't have that muscular chap in the prow of the boat beating his giant drum. But we did have a bloke wearing steel framed spectacles orchestrating our activities in much the same way, through the medium of ferocious briefing sessions. In those days, students in the first and second years of their degree numbered very many hundreds. In the best C P Snow tradition every one of them had weekly written assignments, weekly tutorials, and a weekly laboratory class. Try to imagine a Cambridge college the size of a small town. Even with all of us rowing like maniacs to the beat of those steel framed spectacles, you can see that the arithmetic was against us. The numberless hoards simply overwhelmed us. I did try; I really did. I was commenting on essays, conducting tutorials and holding lab classes from early in the morning (see above) until late at night. We were encouraged to take sleep as necessary. Now before you go saying anything, let me add two things to put your mind at ease. First, I enjoyed it. After the cloistered calm of thesis writing, which is rather a lonely life, I found it incredibly exhilarating. Also – and I accept this is a little sad - I could not think of anything else to do with myself. This is the life for me, I thought. So you see - your sympathy was quite misplaced. There are galley slaves who actually like the drum.

About six months after the Harry Bequest I finished a laboratory class at about nine in the evening. Rather than go home I stayed in my little room, watching the last of the salmon pink Melbourne sunset, reading essays. It must have been about eleven when I thought I'd better stop. The building seemed unusually deserted that evening, even a bit alarming, so I decided to walk down the stairs rather than entomb myself in the lift. I had staggered down to level seven when this mad idea lost its appeal. I pressed the button for the lift and in due course, the bell pinged and the doors opened. I found myself looking at The Prof. I hadn't seen him since that painful conversation about Harry. He nodded, then added, "Good evening, Kennedy." Now you might think this formal style a little stiff. And that's true enough in a place where, "G'day cobber" usually served. But I was pleased he knew who I was. I even took a certain nostalgic pleasure in hearing my name that way. It took me back to school and short trousers, reminding me of those few months before I was permanently addressed as Ken. Schoolboys always prefer the short form, but The Prof was not to know that. I mumbled, "Good evening, Professor", but I doubt he heard me because he had already pressed the button and was busy getting out on the next floor. The closing doors showed him brazenly standing there, waiting for the other lift to come down.

You can't help wondering, can you? On the way down I entertained many hypotheses, some not entirely flattering to myself. Finally, I decided that The Prof, being essentially spirit and naturally invisible, simply could not support being seen wandering about a dark car park like a mortal. I decided to test this hypothesis, taking up a position behind a handy pillar to wait for him to come out. The truth is I was consumed by a desire to know where he went; what he did with himself. Philip

Marlowe minus the fedora about captures the scene. After five minutes spent silently rehearsing a second, "Good evening, Professor," ready for the moment he appeared, I began to feel uneasy. I had intended calling out nonchalantly, as if I were simply passing by but after ten minutes I realised this could well go wrong. The scene was shifting from Chandler to something more in the Hammer Films tradition. It was very late and leaping out from behind a pillar might appear a trifle deranged. I need not have worried - he never reappeared. It was very many years before I realised why.

I think I saw him just once more that first year, apart from a long distance view at a public lecture. It was on the occasion of the departmental group photograph. I still look at this now and then. The Prof has positioned himself in a democratic off-centre position: quite a short chap, wearing a tailored suit with waistcoat (a decided eccentricity in mid-summer Melbourne). A dapper figure, standing extremely erect, steely eyes defying the camera to do its worst. He doesn't look happy. Behind him there is a Paul Nash print he had donated to the common room: not one of the truly unbearable war scenes, but not exactly designed to cheer you up either: bleak about captures it. As he was leaving, he noticed me looking at it and said, "What do you think?" Bear in mind this was only our second exchange since that unfortunate business about Harry. I exclude the conversation in the lift because you have to admit it didn't get very far. I could think of nothing to say. By then this mysterious missing man had started to terrify me. I find it hard to explain – it was to do with the asymmetry of power. In a creepy way, awareness of The Prof was making me look over my shoulder. Incidentally, my own image in that photograph is of an undernourished twelve-year old wearing his first grown up suit. I look as if I am drowning, or possibly have already drowned. I really had tried. Tried my best. But the life academic was taking its toll. Even I couldn't help wishing the chap with the drum would give it a rest now and then.

Shortly after that photograph I got a letter from The Prof. Not damp alcoholic purple but bone dry and sealed in an envelope. It addressed me as "Dear Kennedy" and asked whether I could spare the time to see him. The question was apparently rhetorical because he specified a date and time. It appeared I must wait many days for this ghastly appointment. I showed the letter to my fellow slaves, cunningly hoping I could thereby discover whether they had received something similar. They were only too willing to say none had. The delay augured badly, they said. You need to understand The Prof was not greatly liked. I was told the cruel delay was intended to increase my anxiety. I did not explain to them that there was no room for my anxiety to increase: on any known scale, it had reached its maximum. More, and you would have had to give it another name. An unhealthy calm settled over me in the following days. Walter Raleigh probably felt that way waiting to go down those stone stairs. I rarely saw my wife on account of my tutorial duties, but I did manage to engineer a meeting one weekend, between shifts, as it were. I explained my job was about to end. We agreed it had been an interesting time. I think she added some good might come of it in that she would now see me occasionally. I'm not sure I thought that was compensation enough.

The relentless days went by and the morning of my dismissal dawned as these things do. Sick at heart, I reported to the dragon and was asked to wait. I recall she smiled at me. She had never done that before – an extremely sinister experience. Vapours from her duplicating machine inched my heart rate into an activity known as fibrillation. I sat on, regretting that I knew so little about cardiac arrest. Eventually I was ushered in. The Prof was behind his desk. He also smiled - an experience vastly more sinister. I became aware that I had lost my powers of speech and concluded I had suffered a minor stroke. Or possibly a major stroke - why short change myself? Possibly I was already dead. He started speaking unaware I was considering how bodies might discreetly be shifted off the thirteenth floor in one of those black zip-up bags. I became aware he was trying to catch my attention. I heard him say he had appointed me to a lectureship in the department. He seemed not to expect any kind of response and suggested I talk to one of his colleagues about my future duties. The dragon gave me the contract on the way out. She didn't smile, having used up her quota.

As a lecturer, I saw a bit more of him. I even had lunch with him one day and the event is relevant to the conclusion of this story. I was facing the task of interviewing some undergraduates - applicants for a prize, I think. He wanted to explain how to do it. I will never forget the peculiar intensity he brought to the topic. He insisted that the questions themselves were of less importance than the order in which they were posed and got quite excited pressing this point. I recall being completely baffled as to why.

After a couple of years I decided I wanted to go home. Here's not the place to say why. It was necessary to find a new job and I had no idea at all how you did this. If you've been paying attention to this epic you will have noticed that my jobs up to this point had been provided as a result of angelic intervention. It seemed unreasonable to expect them to keep this up. After thinking about it, the best I could come up with was to write a rather craven letter to the only Important Psychologist I could think of – Donald Broadbent, head of an Applied Psychology Unit at Cambridge. Perhaps you don't know of him - just imagine a god-like being, that should do. It seemed unlikely that god would reply, although oddly enough I felt no urge to write elsewhere. And indeed, there was no reply. Not for about three months, that is, when a letter did arrive; not from the great man himself, but from another lesser eminence, unknown to me. He apologised for the delay, said he had heard from god, and suggested I wrote to a named individual at the University of St Andrews in Scotland, enclosing appropriate letters of recommendation. He urged me to enquire whether a particular post was still available. I copied this form of words, asked two colleagues to write in my support, and duly winged my air mail to Scotland. Three weeks later Scotland replied. The post I referred to had been filled. There was, however, a lectureship vacant. It was assumed this would be of interest and accordingly it was offered to me, subject to a period of probation. So that's how it's done, thought I.

I had to make an appointment to see The Prof and break the bad news. The news I was leaving, that is. Childishly, I felt enormous pleasure in doing this: escaping his all-encompassing grip; breaking free at last. Because this move at least had not involved, could not have involved, The Prof's unseen hand. He knew nothing about it, I was sure of that. It's true he had been at Cambridge University for a while as a student but there was nothing to suggest he had access to the all-powerful subterranean academic network that had mysteriously come to my aid. After all, The Prof was South African: little there to suggest Scottish connections. And hearing these grim tidings was surely going to cause him some grief. I felt grief was in order. Being South African, he would not be familiar with the stirring words of Mr Henley, but I felt like reciting, "In the fell clutch of circumstance I have not winced nor cried aloud. Under the bludgeonings of chance my head is bloody, but unbowed." Something like that, anyway. Fell clutch seemed about right - he really had worked me awfully hard. In the event, the encounter was an anti-climax: he didn't turn a hair. Simply produced one of those quiet enigmatic smiles and wished me well. So there you are – I was captain of my soul at last. You simply don't know the relief I felt getting rid of those bloody angels.

It took me years to discover how wrong I had been about that.

CHAPTER 5

Oscar discovered

THE discovery process started some fifteen years later; in 1979. By then I had moved to distant Scotland and prospered a little, as one does. Queen's College, St Andrews, where my duties began, became the University of Dundee in its own right. In 1972 I became a professor there myself, albeit I was hardly out of short trousers. Exactly how that came about is for another time – although I will say now it is not unrelated to this Oscar saga. Perhaps you recall 1979? That fateful year marked in history by the advent of Mrs Thatcher. It was marked in my university by an advent of its very own, equally cataclysmic: we were saddled with a new Principal, the person they call a Vice Chancellor in England. It seemed I was fated to spend my days under the baleful stare of very strange people. And few came stranger. I think I mentioned the Prof was a little **strange** - this new Principal could have given lessons on the subject.

I am at a dinner. My host is this same Principal. A small gathering in quite an elegant upstairs drawing room. A blokeish sort of affair - few women; cigar smoke even before dinner, a creepy masonic pall hanging over the event. We were in **University House**, overlooking the river Tay. Guest of honour: a professor from Aberdeen called R V Jones. Quite a coup, really, because Jones had just published *Most Secret War*, his best-selling book on military intelligence in WWII. He was basking in fame and royalties. The Principal, proud of his big fish, was keeping him safely in the net, letting the right people have sight of a few scales now and then. Not to touch, you understand. He was an unbearably pompous chap, a bit of a bully and fond of the sound of his own voice. Unfortunately, Professor Jones was much the same, at least with regard to the voice. It looked as if we were in for a night spent watching two old buffers shouting at each other.

Now, as luck would have it, I had that very week read *Most Secret War* and although I'm quite a timid chap (I refer you to my previous chapters) I picked my moment, stiffened my courage, and piped up from a distance to ask the Great Man whether he would tell us his version of the famous Coventry story. To refresh your memory, there was a massive German air raid on Coventry on the night of November 14, 1940. Perhaps, I asked, Professor Jones could give his slant on the story that Mr Churchill had had intelligence about that raid but could not act on it for fear of letting the cat out of the bad. The cat in question being the fact the Enigma Code had been broken. I didn't mention it, but I had a modest interest in the affair, having passed many a wartime night in a cellar not so very far from Coventry. In my special portable cot. Rather inadequately dressed I may add.

An awkward silence fell upon the room, the way it sometimes does when the wrong new voice appears. Professor Jones stared at me as if I'd taken leave of my senses and puffed his cheeks out. I'd only seen that before in films (a little like Alastair Sim in the role of Ebenezer Scrooge). Then he scuttled off to a remote corner of the room like a wounded stickleback, his minder hurrying after to offer *sotto voce* comfort. It must have been about then the dinner table was discreetly re-arranged. When I eventually found it, my chair certainly qualified as being at the table, but located in such a remote latitude that I would have needed the postal service to pose further questions. So I never got to know; secrets and all that. I learned later that journalists were given instructions as to certain words never to be used in front of the good professor - possibly **Coventry** was one of them. I went home fuming, thinking of my cot, resolving to find out for myself the very next day, without fail. Then I went to bed and forgot all about it for about thirty years. I should add, in case you are distressed by all this, my dad so approved of Mr Churchill that he would have considered general incineration an entirely proper contribution to the war effort.

Those thirty years passed. We now reach 2013; I am busy working on my novel *Lucy*, reading a lot about life in Vichy France. I suppose it was inevitable: I stumbled yet again on Coventry. Please understand me, Coventry is in no way relevant to the novel, it's just that memories of that dreadful dinner party came flooding back and well, you know how things are? I starting poking around a bit, thinking I'll just have another go at finding the truth, it won't take long. And before you could say knife I was wondering where the afternoon had gone. You do have to feel sorry for historians, don't you? When you look carefully at the past – even your own past - all you get is a jumble of contradictions. But then, you've read Chapter 2 so I don't need to labour the point. Truth really does lie at the bottom of a very deep well.

I was about to give up my quest, cursing a wasted day, when, in some obscure text, I read this:

> *Wing Commander Oscar Oeser wrote to Jean Howard on Apr 12, 1975: "I do remember REGENSCHIRM. This was obviously going to be a large operation. The code name made me think it must be Birmingham (Chamberlain's umbrella.) But no, Air Intelligence decided it must be London, and all night-fighters and fire brigades concentrated down there. On the night, about midnight, I was on leave in Cambridge, when an endless stream of bombers came over. I feared the worst, couldn't sleep, and went down to the kitchen to brew a cuppa. My hostess ...saw I was upset and perturbed, but I couldn't tell her why, so we put it down to strain of overwork. That was the night of Coventry."*

All thoughts of Coventry vanished. You see, that was his name: Oscar Oeser. This was Oscar! My Oscar, if you like. This was The Prof - the scary man with the enigmatic smile who had given me a job (two jobs if you want to be pedantic). Along with nightmares, that is. How come I didn't know about all this? Wing Commander, for heaven's sake! He never mentioned it.

And why would anybody turn to The Prof for information on British Air Intelligence? What would he know about it? In my galley slave days knowing anything about The Prof's background had been discouraged. We knew he was South African, of course; or possibly German if you wanted to think the worst. Either seemed curse enough to justify his unpopularity. I'm sorry – I really am, as you will discover soon enough - but that was the truth of it: a very hard man to like, was The Prof.

Research on *Lucy* was abandoned forthwith. I set out to discover the truth about Oscar. So long as you bear in mind what I said about truth – here's the best I can do. The first thing to say is the usual sources are no use at all. Oscar died in 1983. There were a few obituaries, but all were vague about what he did in the war. I perked up when I discovered my old department in Melbourne had celebrated its 50th anniversary in 1996 and produced a book to mark the occasion. That would be the place to look, I thought – after all, Oscar founded the place and worked there for twenty-five years: you'd imagine they would remember him. *Au contraire.* He gets a mention of course, but it's not very long, not very informative, and certainly not very kind. After pointing out he worked for a time in Germany with the psychologist Erich Jaensch, the book goes on to say:

> *In his later years Jaensch's writing came to reflect theories of race current in Germany in the 1930s. Watching with horror as his mentor turned into a Nazi sympathiser. Oeser developed a life-long antipathy to fascism. It was an antipathy that would colour Oeser's research interests, if not always his administrative style, in a very tangible manner. When appointed, Oeser was working in Germany in the Personnel Research Section of the Allied Control Commission; he was helping to screen local authorities for inappropriate fascist tendencies. Oeser had what some at the time might have described as a "good war," playing an important role in Allied*

code-breaking efforts and rising to the position of acting Wing Commander.

That's it. There was no more. You can tell they didn't like him, can't you? It would be difficult to compose a more spiteful piece of prose. That phrase, "If not always his administrative style," is not exactly subtle is it? And that poisonous word "acting" attached to his rank? Come to think of it, "inappropriate" fascist tendencies also sounds a bit snide: are there appropriate ones? Alright, confirmation Oscar was not liked; not much else. I cast my mind back to the galley slave years. Did I dislike him all that much? What could I dredge up from the well on that question? He was a scary chap, no doubt about that. Still scary in retrospect. But in my few encounters with him he had actually been quite kind. And he'd given me a job. Surely you have to know someone to dislike them and I hadn't come close to knowing him. Frankly, I began to wonder whether any of us knew him.

Oscar Oeser was born in 1904, in Pretoria, South Africa. His parents were German Jews, his father a goldsmith. The young Oscar was quite prodigiously clever. By the age of twenty-one he had graduated from Pretoria University with a degree in physics and mathematics, completed a Masters degree, and become a university lecturer in physics. We live in timid, post-modern, times and it is considered naïve to imagine really big questions might be tractable. Indeed, university courses are now laid on specially to explain to students that there actually are no big questions or, at least, that all questions are equally big; which must be a little depressing for them. It was not so in Oscar's day. In the 1920s, physics was wrestling with the implications of Quantum Theory; implications that had had an influence far beyond the laboratory, affecting the art, music and literature of the time. And the same was true of another revolutionary theory going the rounds: Sigmund Freud's Theory of the Unconscious was changing the way people thought about themselves -

affecting art, literature, poetry and (particularly) film. I mention Freud yet again to explain what might otherwise seem rather odd – the fact that a student of physics could end up drawn to psychology. But really it should not be all that surprising. Physics teaches you to ask big questions and there are few bigger than the relationship between *things* in the real world and *thoughts* in the mind (or is it in the head?).

How things get turned into thoughts qualifies as a first-rate big question. Indeed, before we start asking, as I did in Chapter 2, what memories are made of, it might have been a good idea to ask what *anything* is made of. Philosophers had been making a decent living out of such questions for millennia and all of a sudden they had to come to terms with a new breed of scientists muscling in. They didn't like it one bit. They grudgingly tolerated physicists, whose work was pretty impenetrable in any case, but they were mightily irked by psychologists, who seemed not to deserve to be scientists anyway. In fact, rather an ugly academic turf war broke out over who had the right to think about certain questions (it's still going on, by the way). Philosophers considered it particularly impudent to imagine that ancient problems like how to relate body and mind might actually be addressed in the laboratory. Nonetheless, Oscar the physicist wanted to be one of this new breed of questioning *scientific* psychologist. His whole life would be determined – and clouded - by that decision.

Where could a bright-eyed bushy-tailed physics graduate, full of youthful enthusiasm for a new world of ideas, realise an ambition to be an experimental psychologist? Certainly not in England: in the 1920s, psychology had barely got started in England. There was only one obvious place: Germany. The first psychological laboratory had been established there; all the exciting work was going on in German or Austrian universities. Oscar spoke German perfectly, so what was he waiting for? That is how, in 1927, he came to arrive at the University of Marburg and register for a doctoral degree in psychology.

The second volume of a book entitled *My Struggle* had just been published. It was the talk of the town, an instant best-seller. The author, Adolph Hitler, was making a name for himself; even his political ambitions were beginning to seem realistic. The book is very long and famously incoherent, but contains some psychologically significant assertions: in particular, the claim that mankind is self-evidently divided into "types." Since he read almost everything, Oscar probably read it. Whether he accepted its thesis is another matter. Professor Erich Jaensch, the celebrated boss of the "Marburg School" of psychology had read it, and certainly did accept it. He wasn't a member of the Nazi party when Oscar arrived, but he had already joined the equally unpleasant *Militant League for German Culture*. So the claim that Oscar would only in his later years watch "with horror as his mentor turned into a Nazi sympathiser," can't be right. He must have been well aware of his mentor's sympathies and either misunderstood their implications (which is unlikely) or somehow found a way to ignore them. This last is not quite so hard to believe as you may think, because a kind of coffee-table fascism was quite the done thing in Marburg at the time; indeed, newspapers and popular literature throughout Europe were almost casually anti-Semitic. I assume Oscar bit his tongue and put up with it. If so, he paid for his naivety.

In his defence, there was nothing inherently racist, much less *fascist*, in the theoretical position adopted by the Marburg School. Like any discovery it was a case of what you wanted to do with it. From a psychological point of view, the claim being made was dramatic: measureable differences in the way people formed visual images could be used to assess personality. Who wouldn't find that idea exciting? Oscar was bitten. Classifying people into *types* was very much the hot topic in psychology. Freud had taken a tentative step in that direction discussing differences in the propensity for neurosis. Jung was to go much further, introducing terms like *extravert* and *introvert* into the language. But those ideas were simply the speculations of clever clinicians. The fascinating thing about the Marburg typology was that it was firmly grounded in something tangible; something that could be measured in the laboratory – namely, differences in the ability to link sensations and ideas. It all hinged on a crucial measurement of the ability to form a special kind of vivid visual impression, called an *eidetic* image. You can well see why all this might intrigue a physics student.

I will give you just a flavour of the approach. Laboratory tests were devised to measure degrees of *synaesthesia*, or the degree to which the senses fused or "bled" into each other. There are quite big individual variations in this. For example, people vary in the degree to which they associate music in a minor key with the colour blue, or associate the colour red with the sensation of heat. Some people exhibit very pronounced synaesthesia. Solomon Shereshevsky, for example, the famous memory man studied by the Russian psychologist Luria, might describe a particular word as "tasting crumbly" or consider a number as having its own peculiar black shape, and so on. The poet Rimbaud associated the vowels with colours: the letter *A* was black, *E* white, *U* green, etc. These were not arbitrary associations; it's hard for us to understand, but apparently he really experienced them that way. Putting the matter very simply, Jaensch and his followers at Marburg considered the type of person whose different senses fused in this way as being at a disadvantage. A poorly differentiated type of person, as he termed it, would be easily distracted, prone to illogical thought, often artistically or musically inclined, but with a poor sense of clock time; disorganised and always late. The Marburg laboratory had completely objective tests which would measure and grade these regrettable propensities. At the other pole of the typology were people whose senses were well differentiated. They were possessed of a reliable inner clock, logical, bent to the task at hand, cognitively stable, and so on. There is more than a hint of a value judgement and you can see where it might lead. An allegedly neutral classification system could easily provide the means for "scientifically" distinguishing, for example, the illogical, effeminate, atheistic, musically-inclined Jew from the logical, iron-clad, warlike Aryan. Indeed, in just a few short years that was precisely what it was doing.

What did Oscar think of all this at the time? We don't know; and his writings offer no clues. My guess is that he clung to the belief that the typology was interesting in itself and need not *necessarily* be put to the service of a burgeoning Nazi ideology. And he would have been right. Almost any other psychological typology could have been put to similar use; perhaps in particular Jung's. A psychological theory isn't, in itself, a political statement. Unfortunately, the more objective and apparently scientific the underlying methodology, the greater the risk that it can be used for political ends. Scientific authority – the cult of the expert - is all too easily deployed by politicians to establish a kind of thoughtless moral high ground and stifle dissent. Lysenko's influence in Stalinist Russia stands as permanent warning to us all. Oscar must surely have found claims about "the Jews" offensive and ridiculous, for obvious reasons. Perhaps the claims were muted at first - he left before the full-blown lunacy broke out.

If you think the term "lunacy" a little over the top, consider a paper Jaensch wrote in 1939: *The Hen-run as a Means of Research and Explanation in Human Race Questions.* He had been impressed by some ethological work on the egg-rolling behaviour of grey-lag geese. I'm sure there are goose-lovers among my readers and I don't want to cause offence, but I claim geese don't have much going for them by way of sophisticated nuances of personality. Nonetheless, Jaensch painstakingly reanalysed these egg-rolling data and convinced himself there was a clear contrast to be made between the slightly delinquent behaviour of a "Southern" type of goose and the more orderly Nordic type (I'm not making this up). Northern chicks pecked steadily and accurately (he doesn't claim they goose-stepped, but I suppose he might have); The Southern sort of goose, manifestly inferior, pecked rapidly, impulsively and inaccurately. Doesn't this, he asked, perfectly reflect racial differences between the restless, lively, overly-flexible Mediterranean type and the calm measured tenacious

Germanic? Sad isn't it? By the outbreak of war, Jaensch was Hitler's favourite psychologist and psychology at Marburg, harnessed to the Nazi ideology, had well and truly taken leave of its senses.

Oscar left in 1931 with his doctorate in psychology and a deep understanding of German scientific psychology. In the introduction to one of his books Jaensch described him as "my friend" and Oscar must have valued this, because he translated the book into English. But I'm sure, little worms of doubt may have been creeping in. He would have noticed the British Society for the Advancement of Science meeting in his far-away home city of Pretoria in 1929. Perhaps he felt a little homesick. He would have read what the President had to say about the Marburg School because it caused quite a stir. Polite, but rather muted, praise was followed by a devastating put-down:

Here are some extremely interesting observations on imagery. Why should we hasten to fashion from them a key to all the most difficult problems of our science? It does seem to be rather in a hurry with its sweeping generalisations.

The speaker was Frederick Bartlett, the man who wrote that book on remembering I mentioned in Chapter 2. Perhaps I'm making too much of it – it's my story, after all – but I think Oscar agreed. That's a guess, but one thing is sure - he left Marburg with his PhD, and promptly enrolled for another one at Cambridge. Under Professor Bartlett's personal supervision.

For many reasons, Cambridge altered the course of Oscar's life. The contrast with Marburg was striking. He had to come to terms with the fact that the fellows and professors considered the discipline of psychology (if they considered it all) as narrowly allied to physics or to physiology. They were clear it should confine its attention to things that could be measured objectively; and equally clear it should eschew speculation like the plague. You can translate that as meaning neither Freud in particular – nor indeed, the mind in general - were to get a look in. If you think this perspective a trifle warped, my reply is that it persists to this day. Psychology will keep trying to creep into the crack between the world of things and the mental world of thoughts; and invariably it is rebuffed. You see, philosophers live there – have done since Plato's time – and there's no room left. There you have it – the curse of psychology: like Adam after the fall, locked out of the garden. Bertrand Russell approved of the Cambridge definition of psychology (well he would, wouldn't he?). Ludwig Wittgenstein was present at the opening ceremony of the new department in 1913, demonstrating apparatus to study rhythm. Oscar duly completed his second PhD (looking at the way people differed in their response to form and colour), but, as we shall discover, he was increasingly unhappy with a discipline that seemed incomplete. Psychology without the mind is like *Hamlet* without the Prince. You can soldier on with it if you like, but increasingly you seem to be answering questions nobody is asking.

CHAPTER 6

Oscar: Cambridge and beyond

YOU'VE noticed we're getting on and he's not a Wing Commander yet. In fact nothing at all so far suggests that direction of travel. The first hints comes with Oscar's life in Cambridge, and the people he met there.

He was a member of Trinity College, the place the best mathematicians tended to go. The topic he settled on for his doctorate – his second doctorate, mind you - was the perception of colour. Some of the imagery tests used in Marburg involved judgements of colour, so he had not set off in a completely new direction. The research would have attracted the interest of a fellow student – somebody who shared Oscar's interest in art; and coincidentally, somebody who had also started out studying mathematics only to change course. In Anthony Blunt's case he had changed in order to study French. You will know Blunt: the willowy aristocratic figure with the effortlessly superior expression: Surveyor of the Queen's pictures, Director of the Courtauld Institute, author of several books on the art of Nicolas Poussin. In Oscar's day, he was still aristocratic, but less elevated. A committed, if rather surprising, disciple of Karl Marx, he had spent time in Germany and would have been drawn to a colleague fresh from the prestigious University of Marburg. Not drawn too far, of course, because Oscar would have no interest in the feverish homosexual clique surrounding Blunt – Oscar preferred girls. At least two members of Blunt's crowd– Kim Philby and Guy Burgess - were also at Trinity in Oscar's day and they would all have dined together regularly. It wouldn't be all that long before he would be working alongside Nigel Burgess, the rather shadowy brother of the flamboyant Guy, but you'll have to wait to discover exactly where. In case you wonder, Donald Maclean arrived only as Oscar was leaving, otherwise he could have told his grandchildren he had spent his youth among the Cambridge Four.

What must they have made of this clever German Jew, newly arrived from a country hurtling towards fascism? Did they even know he was Jewish? It is likely, because they belonged to a class where the question would certainly be posed, if only in private: upper middle class; well connected; snobbish in an unaffected way; not at all awkward with the casual anti-Semitism of their age. Mind you, Anthony Blunt would have been wounded that anyone might think him middle class. Albeit a comrade at heart, he had royal connections, being a distant twig on the Bowes-Lyon family tree. Philby was also not too far from royalty - his father had been an advisor to the King of Saudi Arabia. All Burgess could claim was a stint at Eton, but perhaps that was classy enough for his chums. They were toffs, moving easily among the charmed political circles of 1930s high society, protesting disillusion with the decadence of their parents. Evelyn Waugh's *Vile Bodies*, published in 1930, had them to a tee. Oscar, who had read his Freud closely, would have been amused by these florid manifestations of a guilt complex. You can recognise the same syndrome today – film stars and the pampered children of the well-to-do implausibly expressing solidarity with the down-trodden. There are new causes now, but communism in Oscar's day - in what might be termed its religious manifestation - was the salve of choice for the conscience of the rich. Poorly understood inner guilt coupled with the intellectual challenge of *Das Kapital*: what more could a student demand to pass his days? In our time, the environmental movement, which has points in common with evangelical communism, offers the same intellectual redoubt behind which the rich and powerful can ponder remedies for the misfortunes of others, *de haut en bas*.

In case you were starting to wonder, I am not about to claim Oscar was recruited as a spy. I guess he was sounded out, but to no effect. Nonetheless, you are close – and his story is just as startling. Although you will have to live with a little more bread before I spread the jam. For the moment, just consider how unusual had been his life over the past five years. He had moved in short order from an environment of embryonic fascism into one of embryonic communism. He had seen mass unemployment in Germany usher in totalitarian fascism. But whatever Philby claimed – and I'm sure he went to great lengths to claim it - it really made no sense to see the rise of fascism in Hitler's Germany as a capitalist reaction to socialism. A similar inexorable rise in unemployment in England seemed to presage revolution; it was in the air – at least, in the air at Trinity College, along with the cigar smoke. Was Oscar tempted by the choice Cambridge seemed to hold out? Like a lot of young men of his generation he was faced with a choice in capital letters: Left or Right? He chose neither. He was as repelled by the lazy utopian communism of Cambridge as by the siren calls of fascism in Marburg. The evidence suggests he had no time for the Cambridge revolutionaries discussing remedies to the world's ills over the latest cocktail. As you will see, he found something better to do with his time. The study of types in Marburg had allowed him to see a psychological equivalence between fascism and communism. They had in common charismatic leaders; an all-powerful state acting with impunity; the perversion of science; and terror. I believe he turned away from both.

I can give you a reason for this assertion. It is, of course, written in the rest of his life, but since you have yet to read that, here is a tangible clue to be going on with. In his last year at Cambridge he decided to translate the work of the linguist, Karl Vossler. At first sight this seems a quixotic thing to do. He was working on colour perception, not language, and writing a doctoral thesis is not a cakewalk, even for someone as driven as Oscar. It was going to be a massive distraction. Vossler's book is over 200 pages long, dense with quotations in Latin, Italian and French. Why on earth did he do it? More to the point, why did he choose to do it *then*?

Vossler was a liberal thinker with ideas way ahead of his time concerning the relationship between language and culture. He was, if you like, an early exponent of what we call now the theory of *linguistic relativity* – the idea that the world we experience is very much shaped by our language. All psychology students know about the Whorfian Hypothesis; what they tend not to know is that Vossler had the idea long before Benjamin Whorf was on the scene. I should add, linguistic relativity, even today, is usually treated as heresy. You can date a profound shift in Oscar's thinking from the translation of this book. His theoretical stance became, for want of a better word, decidedly libertarian. Torn between left and right, he ended up in an uncertain middle ground - the position adopted a few years later by Friedrich Hayek, for much the same reasons. You recall Hayek? Something of a hate figure: Mrs Thatcher's favourite economist. Oscar was going to find it a hard row to hoe, having friends on neither side.

Along with a libertarian stance you typically find idealist notions in philosophy, particularly the writings of Kant. This has dramatic consequences for the sort of things you believe psychology can achieve. For one thing, you inevitably begin to doubt that you could ever know what things *really* are. All you can know is what your mind or your language makes of them – and that's not at all the same. Obviously, if you believe that, basing psychology on the measurement of sense impressions seems completely misguided. Yet this is exactly what Oscar had been doing for five years in the course of two doctoral theses. He had argued himself into a position in which neither German behaviourism nor Cambridge psychophysics could possibly underpin the sort of psychology he wanted to practise; the sort that could address big questions. The laboratory suddenly seemed a very unpromising place. It was not a happy position to be in and it coloured the rest of his life.

By the time his Cambridge days were over, Oscar had clocked up an extraordinary list of achievements. He had graduated from universities in South Africa, Marburg and Cambridge, with degrees in three subjects (mathematics, physics and psychology) and in two different languages. He had worked as a university lecturer. He had written two doctoral theses, published several scientific papers and translated the works of both Jaensch and Vossler. He spoke German, English and French fluently and could read Italian well enough to translate Dante. He had a good working knowledge of Latin. He was just twenty-seven years old. And you remember I said he found something better to do with his time than talk of revolution. He joined the RAF Volunteer Reserve squadron at Cambridge and learned to fly, securing his full pilot's licence at Duxford airfield in August 1931. He was going to need it.

As he left Cambridge, an inconspicuous chap was arriving: the son of a Scottish ironmonger, not out of the same box as our four Cambridge spies. He had a degree already (albeit from Glasgow University, which I imagine hardly counted). John Cairncross came to Cambridge to study French and German, alongside Blunt at Trinity College. He was recruited to become the most celebrated soviet agent of his time. His long anonymity as the "Fifth Man" sounds like the stuff of legends; the truth is less glamorous. Cairncross was among those responsible for giving England's atomic secrets to the Russians. Oscar will certainly meet him before this story has ended.

There was another arrival that final year, just as he was presenting his doctoral thesis. A shy undergraduate called Alan Turing, having been rejected by Trinity to study mathematics, took up a place at King's as second best. He probably didn't meet Oscar then, but they will certainly meet before this story has ended.

CHAPTER 7

The School Teacher

OSCAR did not go back to South Africa. Rather, as a very public declaration of his libertarian leanings (he was young, after all) he joined the staff of an "experimental" school called Dartington Hall in Devon and became a teacher. This decidedly unorthodox establishment with progressive principles seemed the perfect match for the formidably qualified Dr Oeser. You had to be brave to consider Dartington for your offspring in 1931. That is, you might think twice before sending little Hilary to a mixed-sex boarding school with no formal classrooms, no uniforms and a peculiar democratic ethos. No corporal punishment, what's more: an educational heresy if ever there was one. But it was just the place for a somewhat disillusioned young Oscar to experiment with his libertarian views on education, trying to understand the psychological dynamic between pupil and teacher. It was just the place to find ways of applying a broad and humane psychology to teaching and instruction. He was there for a brief two years (although in that time he did manage to get married twice). The evidence suggests he enjoyed himself enormously.

Dartington Hall had rapidly gained a reputation as the place to send the wayward children of the intelligentsia. Among the boarding pupils in Oscar's time was little Lucian Freud, grandson of Sigmund. He had left Berlin with his parents, the family more aware of the Nazi threat than was grandfather, still clinging on in Vienna in the belief his reputation would be adequate protection. Oscar was one of a long line of schoolmasters who tried to tame the unruly Lucien with little success.

It was the custom at Dartington Hall to produce a regular bulletin called *News of the Day*. Number 441 issued on Tuesday 11th July 1933, read:

Notices –

The Dartmoor Otter Hounds are meeting on 13th July at the Seymour Hotel.

Congratulations to Dr Oscar Oeser on his appointment as Lecturer in Psychology and head of the department of Experimental Psychology, University of St Andrews.

Yes, I know, I know: the conclusion of Chapter 4 is coming back to bite me – you must have expected something like that. Far from knowing nothing at all about St Andrews, Oscar had actually worked there. He must have known Donald Broadbent from his Cambridge days. I suppose letters were exchanged. It must have been Oscar's intervention that got me that job. I blush to think of that: there had been angels after all.

I should clear up one thing about this Notice. The bit about the otters is probably correct, I have no way of checking; but the rest is something of an exaggeration. There was actually no "department" of Experimental Psychology in St Andrews at that date, just an honours course taught by two lecturers: one based in St Salvator's College, the other in University College, Dundee, then part of the university. The man running the show was Professor Stout, certainly a psychologist by profession, but actually employed as a philosopher. Oscar was to fill the St Salvator's post, its title having only that year been changed from "lecturer in logic and metaphysics" to "lecturer in experimental psychology". His predecessor had managed to establish some rudimentary laboratory facilities in the cloisters of the Chapel, but Marburg it was not.

There is no record as to how Oscar came to get this job so I'm going to speculate a little. It was surely the work of Frederick

Bartlett. He had recently become a professor in Cambridge and was learning to flap his wings. The hostility from philosophers in the ancient universities towards the infant discipline of psychology had been something to behold and having secured his chair, Bartlett wanted to get his own back (I'm sure he had a more elegant way of putting it). We know he set out to determine, or at least influence, all senior appointments in psychology in the country, thereby shaping the nature of the discipline into a characteristic British style. In large measure, he succeeded. It is plausible that Bartlett suggested the St Andrews job to Oscar, and – because that's the way the academic tail gets wagged - Bartlett who lobbied Professor Stout for him to get it.

Alas, it did not turn out at all well. It was the same old story, this time with a twist of peculiarly Scottish lemon. The resident philosophers in St Andrews claimed that psychology could not possibly be an empirical science; it followed, the title of Oscar's lectureship was simply a grotesque category error. He wasn't going to get any help from the resident hard scientists either. They thought the idea of "experimental" psychology quaint or presumptuous, depending on how benevolent they felt. Psychology was pig in the middle again, although I must say Oscar himself didn't exactly court popularity with his colleagues. He blithely introduced Freud into the curriculum and began teaching aspects of psychoanalysis, one of his new passions. If he had offered a course in devil-worship it would have had much the same effect.

You will think I'm exaggerating the vehemence of these ancient academic disputes, but I'm not. I'll call Eric Trist as a witness. Trist - one of the founders of the Tavistock Institute for Social Research, a clinical psychologist, a social anthropologist: a hugely influential figure in the development of applied psychology. Late in his life he wrote an autobiography with the endearing title, *Guilty of Enthusiasm*. He had started out studying English Literature at Cambridge and then moved to do postgraduate work in psychology. He had also been supervised by Bartlett. After graduating, he spent a period in the USA, seeing the depression at first hand and acquiring a social conscience. Acquiring also an unfortunate "enthusiasm" for psychoanalysis. Here's what he writes:

> *When I returned to England in 1935 I had a hell of a time. Just before I came back, Bartlett had sent one of his people to tell me that there was no job for me in psychology in Britain, not even a corner in Cambridge, nowhere! I knew Bartlett had control of all the appointments in psychology in England.*

During his time in the States Trist had witnessed the violence of a textile worker's strike in which several workers had been killed. He had joined the Hunger and Strike Committee in support of strikes in Connecticut. He had even, rather reluctantly, begun to read Marx - finding the analysis of society "made sense", albeit "Wittgenstein had convinced us that metaphysics was 'nonsense'." He goes on:

> *Then I got a break. Oscar Oeser, whom I had met in 1932 in Cambridge, had got some money from the Pilgrim Trust for interdisciplinary work on long-term unemployment in a Scottish area. Oeser interviewed me for the job of social psychologist in his three year project, and was interested in my political experiences of the Depression. Oscar Oeser was a committed academic and an action researcher who wanted to study unemployment and was a very enlightened social democrat at that time.*

The "Scottish area" he mentioned was Dundee, on the Northern bank of the River Tay. You would have been hard pressed to find a better place to study unemployment than Dundee. The inter-war depression had hurt that East coast city very badly. Men had been killed or wounded in such terrifying numbers during WWI that women had taken on many of the traditional masculine working roles in the jute spinning mills. They were badly exploited. Jobs were very scarce. The pay was pitiful. They had no Trade Union. Working life was brutish and often short, on account of industrial diseases (severe deafness and a form of motor ataxia, known unkindly as the "weaver's jig"). Housing conditions for the workers in 1930s Dundee were unspeakably bad – "cruel habitations" as one writer described them. There was chronic youth unemployment. An air of hopelessness pervaded the place. Children frequently went barefoot to school. Corporal punishment was pervasive and singularly barbaric. Indiscipline, very broadly defined, was punished with beatings using a long leather strap, known as a *tawse*. Children were also routinely strapped for academic failure. Oscar, fresh from Dartington, found the situation shocking and depressing – a reaction which, in turn, irked his colleagues in St Andrews, who rather wished their psychology lecturer would find something more becoming to do with his time than study the Dundee under-class.

Research on the causes and consequences of social deprivation and unemployment was atypical of the psychology of that time (to put it mildly). Indeed, in 1936 "unemployment" would be considered a provocative, even subversive, topic for a psychologist to tackle. The political classes were well aware that National Socialism had come to power through an appeal to the unemployed. George Orwell's *The Road to Wigan Pier* was published just as Oscar's project got underway. Orwell (an Old Etonian dossing down incognito over the tripe shop in Wigan) empathised strongly with the working class; his amateur research had attracted the attention of the Special Branch. How the good burghers of St Andrews University must have prayed Oscar would leave well alone.

Perhaps unsurprisingly, the outcome of the Dundee Project was not widely distributed; you can find few traces of the results now. The Dundee work is known largely for its contribution to methodology and in this Oscar was far ahead of his time. He was among the first to argue that psychologists acting as observers should not be apart from their subjects, brandishing notebooks and cameras, but integrated into the community under study.

He must have had that in mind when, years later, he was to send an infant lecturer off to interview a bunch of students. Oscar called the procedure "functional penetration." Whether it could realistically have been employed in Dundee at that time is a moot point. It's a struggle to imagine those well meaning English academics plausibly integrating with unemployed Dundonians, tough fourteen-year olds in the main, vainly looking for a job in the mill. Newcomers usually find the Dundee patois impenetrable. What is clear, however, is that Oscar at this point in his career abandoned experimental psychology and become, in Trist's phrase an *action researcher*. So far as I know, he never again conducted laboratory research. He had become, probably without intending it, a social psychologist.

CHAPTER 8

Telling lies

WHEN war broke out, Oscar's second wife, an Australian, took their two children off to the comparative safety of Melbourne. His lectureship at St Andrews was suspended to allow him to take a commission in the RAF - he never went back, and the university apparently made no effort to woo him. At around that time, Oscar's name came to the attention of Alistair Denniston, possibly through the intervention of Frederick Bartlett, who was involved in a number of secret war-related projects in Cambridge. Denniston was the sort of anonymous character who floats to the top in the British establishment, not particularly good at anything, but with good connections. He was at that time (and until 1942 when Churchill sacked him) in charge of "Room 40" in the Admiralty, an establishment set up during WWI to decrypt the enemy's cyphers. Set up against some opposition, because it had been thought not quite the done thing to read another chap's correspondence. By Oscar's day, Room 40 had become the Government Code & Cypher School, the grandfather of GCHQ.

You only need to look back at Oscar's background to see why Denniston would be interested. Apart from his obvious intelligence, his science training, and his many formal qualifications, he had a complete mastery of the German language and had worked at a professional level as a translator. Plainly, he also knew a lot about human psychology and the way it might be harnessed in time of war. Crucially, he had had recent first-hand experience of Nazi science. It wasn't long before Oscar was taking the train to Bletchley Park to become a code breaker.

Denniston's recruiting methods were unorthodox. He approached suitable people in the University, suggesting they might be interested in a short course then, when they arrived, sized them up for a possible job as code breakers. He sought clever, focused people, with an interest in intellectual puzzles: good chess players; people who solved the Times crossword quickly – you know the kind. Cambridge was the only university that interested Denniston – a rule of thumb that served perfectly well at one level because the place was full of first rate mathematicians, Trinity College in particular. At another level you can see there was quite a serious hidden problem. The gilded generation he was recruiting – the idealistic young men of Trinity – actually despised their stuffy hidebound class-ridden rulers. Denniston would have been surprised (he didn't do "shocked") to learn they thought the Russian revolution had set an example the world should follow and the English version could not come swiftly enough. As we know, all too many of them were willing to help it on its way: that is how Trinity College spies like Maclean, Burgess, Philby and Cairncross ended in the heart of government; and spy-masters like Blunt and Klugman found themselves with extraordinary access to power.

Before I explain what Oscar did at Bletchley Park, I will say just a little about code breaking. Not much, I promise; but we need the context. Two months before the outbreak of war Denniston had attended a meeting in Warsaw with his opposite numbers in the French and Polish cryptographic services. At this meeting, members of the Polish Cipher Bureau explained how, in principle, the German Enigma cipher could be broken.

It is worth dispelling a few potent myths surrounding Enigma. First, the machines themselves were not particularly mysterious; they had been around since the end of WWI and were even used commercially. Second, despite our fond beliefs, the German cryptographic service was more sophisticated than its English opposite number (they had, after all, invented the thing). Finally, although it is often claimed the German High Command was completely unaware Enigma had been broken, this is to misrepresent things a little. The vulnerability of the coding method was perfectly well understood – both Admiral Dönitz and Field Marshal Rommel, for example, suspected signals traffic was being intercepted. The fact the machines were repeatedly modified suggests that these suspicions were taken seriously. The modifications were successful at a technical level, eventually rendering the code unbreakable for all practical purposes. If correct operational procedures were followed, an Enigma machine with five wheels changed on an hourly basis, the output cross-patched at random, produced cipher that was impossible to crack in a realistic timeframe (that is, in hours rather than months). The German error lay in their belief that that was only one way, and that it was simply not worth trying. Turing did not agree and the people at Bletchley Park broke the code to devastating effect. Since Oscar was involved, I will briefly explain how.

The enigma machine is quite simple in concept. Pressing successive letters at a typewriter keyboard allows an electric contact to advance a train of gears or "wheels" each with 26 teeth – one for each letter. Teeth on the wheels themselves are electrically cross-wired and can be set into any one of 26 starting positions. The wheels themselves can be slotted into the machine in a number of different orders. The re-routed electric current illuminated an enciphered letter on a lamp-board which was written down and eventually sent using Morse code. To decipher, the person at the receiving end simply set a machine up in exactly the same initial state and typed in the coded letters. Because the code is reversible, the original plain text now appears on the lamp-board. An extremely ingenious idea.

Enigma machines have weaknesses: the most significant is the fact that a letter cannot be encoded as itself; also, the enciphered code is not strictly random. You can work this out from first principles. A basic Enigma machine had three rotating wheels, so a given letter can be encoded in 26 x 26 x 26 x 6 different ways (the 6 comes from the fact you can slot the three encoding wheels, like a train of gears, in six different orders). That comes to a big number (about 100,000), but if you automate the process at high speed you can obviously work through all the combinations. In fact, that is exactly what the Poles had done and they gave Denniston details of a machine to carry out the task. The Germans were well aware of the vulnerability and, long before war broke out, had added extra wheels and made the machine more secure by "crossing" connections using a system of plug-in cables, scrambling the entry and exit points for ten randomly chosen letters. With five wheels, you now have 26 x 26 x 26 x 26 x 26 multiplied by 60 (to account for all the possible wheel orders) – and about 40 million, million, possible cross-patching arrangements. The odds have now shifted against you - that's the hell of a big number. German cryptographers knew the Enigma code could be broken using the same Polish method, but it was now only a theoretical possibility. That is, you could still test all the possible combinations, but you would not live long enough to arrive at an answer. They concluded – and they were correct - that breaking the code by brute force was not worth the effort because the operational significance of any particular message would have expired (along with the code breaker) long before it could be read.

So how come it was broken? It's the usual story: not the machine's fault, but the people operating it. The fact that a letter cannot be encoded as itself can be exploited unless the operator avoids certain practices. For example, however routine, messages should not always begin the same way because code breakers will guess these ritual initial phrases (or obtain them by other means). If, day after day, weather reports from a particular station begin, "Here is the weather forecast from Station X for the next twenty-four hours," those initial characters provide the key to the door. You now know what the first sixty or so characters of an encoded message mean. You can line these characters up alongside the code produced from a particular wheel setting and check for cases where the same letter occurs in the same place. Since an enigma machine cannot code a letter as itself, you can be sure that particular wheel setting was *not* used.

Such fragments of certainly known (or plausibly guessed) text were known as *cribs*. They were mostly obtained by monitoring the casual chit-chat between operators. Once you knew exactly what a small part of a stream of apparently random letters meant, the odds tipped dramatically in your favour. The number of wheel settings where the cipher for a given crib never produced a repeated letter was vastly smaller than the number of all possible settings. In fact, if the crib was long enough (40 characters might do) the odds shifted from being astronomical to something more like horse race odds - small enough to make testing all possible alternatives a completely practical option again.

This grossly simplified account is in essence what the Bletchley code breaking factory did with Enigma. The unsung heroes were the signals intelligence operators who monitored enemy traffic to discover cribs and identify other useful breaches of operating procedure that could be used to guess plausible wheel settings. Thereafter, the process was automated by arranging Enigma machines in a daisy chain, each feeding the next, testing all the possible combinations until a hit was found. The Germans believed the number of settings to be tested would run to hundreds of millions; in practice it was a tiny fraction of that. The success rate was amazing: in Oscar's section, the main *Luftwaffe* cipher (called RED at Bletchley Park) was actually broken every single day from 1940 to VE Day, usually by eight o'clock in the morning.

The German cryptologists devised operating procedures that should have pretty well eliminated cribs, but they were frequently ignored in the turmoil of day to day operational stress. For example, it is fatally informative to code breakers if a message is repeated without changing the wheel settings. But wireless transmission of Morse is often noisy and messages in the real world have to be repeated more often than not. Although the penalties for breach of operational procedure were severe (death in some cases) operators often had no option but to cut corners. When lives hinge on it and the order is, "Send that again," you simply may not have time to look up a new initial wheel order in the Code Book for the day, reset the wheels in the machine, communicate the new settings, and resend the message.

The code breaking of concern to us went on in Hut 6 at Bletchley Park. Oscar spent the years until 1944 working in the adjoining Hut 3, eventually becoming Head of the section. Breaking the code was only half the job – Oscar's job was to translate the deciphered German text, decide whether it was important or not, relate it to a multitude of other messages, and pass it on. All these time-critical tasks had to be completed at speed, because the information had to reach a command level in time for someone to act on it - otherwise, code breaking itself is no more than an intellectual indulgence. Oscar did this job for four years, in conditions of great secrecy and under relentless pressure. A digest was sent by despatch rider to Churchill's office every day and the British War Cabinet sometimes saw German battle orders before they reached the relevant enemy stations in the field.

It is generally accepted that the stream of "Ultra" information provided by Bletchley Park influenced the on-going war effort decisively. There are literally thousands of accounts of this secret war, including that by the sensitive Professor Jones we met in Chapter 5. Thirty years after the war's end, code breakers secured permission, one by one, to tell their bit of the story. Curiously, all these authors, hurrying to publication, saw themselves as central to the business - a pivotal character, without whom the war might well have been lost. Their squabbles over priority and disagreements about details continue to this day and are not always very edifying; history does tend to be rather a messy business. In the end, your regard increases for those, like Oscar, who did the job and generally kept quiet about it afterwards. Perhaps he could scarcely believe what had befallen him. After all, he wasn't a professional soldier. He must have pinched himself sometimes, wondering how an academic physicist-turned-psychologist, interested in the minutiae of colour perception, ended up at Bletchley Park helping to win World War II. Or perhaps I should make the claim more modest: helping to win my bit of the war - not that he knew I existed, you understand. But without Ultra the destruction of Rommel's supplies in the Mediterranean would not have occurred, changing the course of the North African campaign; my Uncle Ken would not have lived to tell his tale. Without Ultra, German U-boat Wolf Packs would have destroyed shipping conveys in the North Atlantic with impunity and my Uncle Arthur would not have come home. Without Ultra, targets for bombing raids on England would not have been available to Civil defence forces. My father would probably have perished. Neither Churchill in his bunker, nor Alan in his cot, would have been faced with their own particular Coventry dilemma. Without Ultra – in some small way without Oscar - the disposition of the German Air Force before the siege of Kursk would have been unknown to Stalin. The Russians would have lost. The Swastika may well have flown over Buckingham Palace. For want of a nail, as the saying goes.

Oscar was not a spy but he inhabited a world of secrets and deception. If the information reconstructed in Hut 3 was secret, the *manner* of its reconstruction was even more secret. That is the nub of the Coventry question. Code breakers lived in a secret world and sometimes the decision as to how to act on particular information became difficult to distinguish from espionage. There is one supreme example of this. A turning point in the war - one which challenged the allegiances of spies and counter-spies on all sides - Operation Barbarossa , what one commentator called the "greatest military operation in history." In June 1942, at Hitler's personal initiative, a massive German force invaded Russia. Stalin was well aware he would be betrayed eventually. He expected an attack, but had calculated this would only occur after the fall of England (illustrating his superior grasp of strategy). In the weeks running up to the assault, Stalin received warnings from many different sources. In particular, intelligence reports from code breakers in Sweden, who had also penetrated Enigma, gave him the anticipated date of the attack. Stalin treated the news as crude disinformation. Oscar's group in Hut 3 had even better information than the Swedes regarding the intentions of the *Luftwaffe*. They also knew the date of the attack; they knew the precise disposition of German forces. Churchill even sent a personal warning to Stalin through diplomatic channels, only to have it dismissed as a propaganda trick. Stalin claimed the massed forces on Polish territory were simply a feint - the British were just trying to foment discord between allies to protect their own interest. Some have argued that the Bletchley Park information was relayed to Stalin through British double agents in Lucerne, part of the shadowy "Lucy" spy ring. But however well-baited the hook, Stalin was not biting. He remained unconvinced until the morning tanks crossed the border.

Working alongside Oscar in Hut 3, just after operation Barbarossa, was John Cairncross – the man we met in the previous chapter. The Fifth Man. For almost a year at Bletchley Park, Cairncross worked as a Soviet agent. It was standard practice for the original deciphered German-language text to be destroyed by burning once Oscar and his people had translated it. Cairncross devised a way of intercepting these messages and retaining items of interest. He stuffed them in his underwear and rearranged himself later in the train station lavatory. The information was then passed to his Russian controller. As a consequence, Russia was certainly aware Enigma had been broken, although possibly unaware of the scale of the operation. Apart from decoded *Luftwaffe* messages, Cairncross gave the Russians copies of Turing's notes on cryptography and details of the Polish machine used to solve Enigma. It is always possible, of course, in a place built on lies and deception, that the material Cairncross stole was what he was intended to steal. After all, Russia was now more ally than enemy and the code breakers were always looking for plausible cover stories to account for otherwise inexplicable military successes: perhaps Cairncross was less a spy than an unwitting conduit – we may never know. Curiously, he was never prosecuted, not even after publishing his exploits in detail.

If you look in the Kew archives you will discover that around the time of Operation Barbarossa, Wing Commander Oeser was giving a series of lectures at Bletchely Park with the enigmatic title, "Fish." Since 1940, the code breakers had been faced with a completely new, and apparently impenetrable, code. Possibly as a response to the insecurity of Enigma, the Germans had adopted a completely different cypher technique, vastly more secure. It was based on the teletype "Baudot" code – characters represented by punched holes arranged in five columns across a strip of paper tape. Western Union Telegraph messages had been sent that way since the 1860s.

In 1918 an American named Gilbert Vernam suggested an ingenious way of enciphering teletype text by combining the punched tape with a second tape containing randomly placed holes (imagine them overlaid in a particular way). Once the two patterns were combined, the end product could not be broken. You have, in fact, every code breaker's nightmare: the equivalent of the spy's "one-time" pad. What was clever about Vernam's idea was that an encoded message was deciphered simply by combining it a second time with the same random tape. Special rules of arithmetic restored the original message.

In practice, there is no need for an actual second tape – all you need is a machine to add punch holes at random at the sender's end and the same machine at the other end to subtract them. The Germans devoted their formidable cryptographic skills to making machines that would generate these "nearly random" codes. Not truly random, of course - otherwise you would not be able to reproduce it at the other end – but sequences so long they might as well be random. Machines that did this were referred to in Bletchley as *Fish*, and the signal traffic generated from different places was given distinctive fish names – Tunny, Sturgeon and so on.

Fish represented a major problem for the code breakers at Bletchley Park; breaking it made Enigma seem like child's play. Above all, the code breakers were hampered by the fact they had never seen one of these secret German machines. Nonetheless, *Fish* was broken. More than that, the precise construction of the secret machine was deduced, taking the form of a logical wiring diagram, without ever having seen it – a quite extraordinary achievement.

CHAPTER 9

Fishing

SUCCESS breaking *Fish* teletype traffic still depended on operator error to provide cribs. Happily, the Germans obliged in spectacular fashion: a message of 4000 characters was repeated in its entirety, the operator abbreviating things the second time round when the chance arose. Comparison of the two versions together with some inspired statistical analysis of the structure of the two slightly different enciphered messages by Alan Turing produced plausible guesses as to the logical structure of the machine that had encoded them. True, it was a large number of plausible guesses, but not unreasonably large because, unknown to the Germans, British Post office engineers had constructed a machine that tested vast numbers at extremely high speed. Originally using electro-mechanical relays to do the work, this improbable device was eventually recreated in an electronic form, producing Colossus, the world's first programmable computer. German cryptographers knew it was patently absurd try to break a code by testing tens of millions of possibilities. They relied completely on this absurdity and they were seriously wrong to do so: with the aid of cribs, Turing and the British Post Office proved them wrong.

In the latter stages of the war, more and more sophisticated German coding machines of this kind came into use. One in particular generated extremely long sequences of teletype code before repeating itself, producing enciphered messages (nicknamed "Thrasher") that were rarely broken at Bletchley Park. All that could be deduced was that a device of the same general form was being used.

In fact, Thrasher code was produced by the last of a long series of machines built by Siemens & Halske, their use restricted to the High Command, including Hitler himself, then holed up in his Berlin bunker. On April 25th 1945 Hitler, no doubt in rather a depressed state, got news of a raid carried out by RAF Lancaster bombers on his beloved alpine fortress at Berchtesgaden. Houses belonging to Göring and Bormann had been flattened, but his Eagle's Nest retreat had somehow remained intact. He despatched Admiral von Puttkamer to Berchtesgaden with orders to destroy private papers and to safeguard (by burying them) a number of the coding machines kept in mobile radio trucks in the vicinity.

These mobile machines were part of a private communications network operated by Göring; in late April they had been in continuous use for days. Whole books have been written about the fact the traffic was directed to South American agents, using relay stations in Spain or Portugal. These messages have come to play a role in a number of conspiracy theories; in particular the bizarre contention that Hitler somehow survived his ordeal in the bunker (which involved shooting himself), living on as a rather crotchety OAP in a lake-side villa in Patagonia. Notwithstanding this nonsense, the fact the encrypted messages could not be broken was an embarrassment – something dramatic was called for.

Although it was technically still a shooting war in Europe, geopolitical considerations were already shaping priorities as to the identity of the true enemy. Germany had been crushed; Hitler was dead; his close associates were either dead, on the run, or in captivity. The new and urgent concern was to contain the expansionist ambitions of Stalin, albeit still technically an ally. The race was on in Germany to capture as much human and physical capital as possible before it fell into the hands of a new Cold War enemy. Second only to Hitler's nuclear programme, German cryptographic equipment was a priority; in particular the Siemens & Halske machines that Bletchley Park had copied in the abstract, but never actually seen. A commando raid on Berchtesgaden was planned with the aim of capturing the equipment Puttkamer had been sent to protect.

The raid was the idea of Commander Ian Fleming, then a naval intelligence officer, yet to write his series of partly autobiographical books about James Bond. Fleming was a larger-than-life character, running what amounted to a tiny private army known variously as 30 Assault Unit or simply as "Fleming's Red Indians." He suggested a mission to be executed by one of the Anglo-American teams being put together to liberate enemy equipment. There were several of these so-called Target Intelligence Committees, or TICOMs. Team 1 was about to complete possibly the most valuable intelligence raid in WWII. The man placed in command was Wing Commander Oscar Oeser.

In the early days of May, 1945, there was a rather infantile competition going on among the victors to be the first to set foot on Hitler's Eagle's Nest – the newsreel symbol of Nazi power. It was going to be, as journalists are wont to say, an iconic moment. As the historian Stephen Ambrose put it: *Everybody wanted to get there — French advancing side by side with the 101st, British coming up from Italy, German leaders who wanted to get their possessions, and every American in Europe.* It is usually claimed that General "Iron Mike" O'Daniel won the race, pulling down Hitler's Swastika banner on May the 4th or 5th (although I rather think he had to hoist it up first). The date is disputed because the scramble to be first descended into farce when men from a US Airborne Division and men from a French Armoured Division both tried to cross a narrow iron bridge at the same time. Neither would give way. The Americans no doubt resented their come-lately ally turning up at all, but the French, led by General Le Clerk stood their ground, petulantly blocking the path until their claim to plant the French flag over the hated *Berghof* was accepted. In the end, the Stars and Stripes and the Tricolore were flown together, although the only French flag anyone could find was too heavy and kept sliding down

They could well have added the Union Jack, because Hitler's nest was also liberated by Oscar and his TICOM team. They had driven from Paris, probably setting out on May 6th persuading American infantrymen to disguise their vehicles en route with US white stars. On arrival, amid scenes of indiscriminate looting, they isolated Admiral von Puttkamer's forty SS troops and disarmed them - without too much fuss, given that hostilities were about to cease in any case. They took possession of the Siemens & Halske encoding machines and also captured a convoy of four signal trucks equipped with *Fish* machines. The trucks turned out to be Field Marshal Kesselring's secret communications train. A few days later, the TICOM team persuaded their German guests to dig up the recently-buried cache of equipment. No doubt preferring imminent British to Russian hospitality, the German operators even set the equipment up and gave a demonstration.

Oscar also discovered a very advanced electronic device capable of intercepting Soviet teleprinter traffic: messages Bletchley Park had so far failed to break. Russian cryptographers had perfected a way of splitting up encoded messages into nine separate parts and transmitting them in parallel on different wireless channels. The Bletchley Park code breakers had proved powerless to penetrate the messages; this unexpected secret device (promptly nicknamed the "Russian Fish") reconstructed the signals, which could then be broken relatively easily.

At the end of the mission, Oscar's team had captured over seven tons of signals equipment, to be shared out between British and American team members. Details of some aspects of the haul remained secret until 2012; other details may still be secret. They were secrets Oscar had no option but to keep: he lived with them for many years – although not long enough to see the embargo lifted.

He flew back to Bletchley armed with a pass declaring that he had been *Entrusted with the mission of conveying to the United Kingdom certain items of captured enemy equipment of a vital and most secret nature.* The equipment in question was the captured Russian Fish – one prize not shared with the Americans. For the next four years, at a site not far from Bletchley Park, German technicians under British control intercepted Russian signals traffic. Thanks to Oscar, and probably unknown to the Russians, a great deal of secret Soviet military signals traffic was broken in the early days of the cold war.

CHAPTER 10

Le Tri

OSCAR'S war was not yet over. In some ways, it had barely started. Post-war Germany was an ideological void which three of the four victorious nations hoped to shape in different ways (the fourth victor, France, was more concerned with recouping the penal costs levied by their uninvited German lodgers). Psychoanalytic analyses of the Nazi mindset had started to appear and Oscar read these. Understandably, the tone was pessimistic, sometimes extremely so. Interest in Eros, the dominant theme of the frothy indulgent days of pre-war psychoanalysis, had been replaced by Thanatos. Attention turned to little understood instinctive forces driving man towards death and destruction. Psychologists found themselves in the spotlight. Wasn't psychology supposed to deal with human mentality? How come it had failed to predict these horrors? It was, of course, too late to explain that psychologists had put off thinking about the mind, let alone human mentality.

Nonetheless, the key questions were incontestably psychological. Can a whole country be in some sense psychologically diseased? If so, it surely falls to psychologists to identify the pathology; who else could undertake the task? Perhaps, as Nietzsche hinted, there was something peculiarly German in the will to power. Was German militarism, as even some theologians were claiming, incurable? Books appeared, many with Jewish authors, asking how the monstrous excesses of the Nazis were to be understood. What constellation of forces could lead a whole population to complicity in unspeakably inhuman acts? Can a political movement corrupt humanity to that extent? Or is there, after all, some vicious mole of nature in man? Does the Nazi seed lie dormant in us all? What was to become of Germany?

Oscar could never have imagined the narrowness and inadequacy of "experimental psychology" was going to be exposed so soon and in such a cruel context. If the discipline of psychology was to *act*, rather than *talk*, it had to change: the theoretical certainties of the Marburg School seemed ludicrous; psychophysics seemed simply irrelevant. The long-standing European concern with *nature* was seen for what it was – an essentially pessimistic conservative doctrine that had unwittingly come to the aid of the worst kind of fascist ideology. With their victory, the Americans had won more than a territorial war. In the battle of ideas, an emphasis on *nurture* now held sway. Only a few years earlier, Cambridge or St Andrews would have dismissed human motivation as a hopelessly ill-defined topic for psychological analysis. Now, the exigencies of the European situation had placed it centre stage. Aggression in man and other animals became an eminently suitable subject for research. Psychologists lost interest in perception and began studying personality. The person was well and truly back at the centre of the discipline. Oscar, the *action researcher* who had tried to study the psychological consequences of unemployment in Dundee, against the implacable opposition of his colleagues, must have felt vindicated.

Here was the practical question he faced: what on earth do you do with a population – even war-weary and starving – most of whom had recently declared undying allegiance to a kind of devil worship? How could you conceivably build a civil society out of what a later author would call Hitler's "willing executioners"? Of course, one kind of answer became available at Nurenberg, but decisions there were in the framework of legal process. Obviously, individuals whose actions had put them beyond all redemption could be dealt with by the ritual of law. But that was the easy part. What of the others – huge numbers of others – where lip-service to the Nazi creed had been the only way to survive? How can you distinguish the real from the pretend monster? Which is the good, and which the bad, German? Viewed from this distance in time, these questions appear simplistic, even naïve. It was not the case in 1945. If any kind of functioning civil society was to be established, what the French call *un tri* – a sorting – had to occur. And perhaps uniquely in the history of our discipline, it was accepted that only psychologists – ready or not - could undertake the task.

Within a matter of weeks, while the smoke was still rising, American and British de-Nazification programmes and Assessment Centres were established. The principal organisation in the British occupied zone was the German Personnel Research Branch, located at Bad Oeynhausen, probably because that was where Field Marshall Montgomery had taken up residence. Their purpose was clear – one might say, impossibly clear - to determine from among those key personnel remaining alive, those psychologically and intellectually capable of building a new State and working constructively in it. And, of course, to determine who was not, with all the consequences that implied. It was an operation without parallel, for which the discipline of psychology was ill prepared. The person placed in overall command of the British programme was Wing Commander Oscar Oeser.

Oscar would not have sought this job, but he was the obvious choice. For one thing, there cannot have been many high-ranking intelligence officers with doctoral qualifications in psychology from a German university, capable of conducting challenging psychiatric interviews in German. But far more significant than Oscar's qualifications was another fact - he was one of very few British psychologists at that time who would have considered the task even remotely possible.

Oscar ended his war selecting people fit to run the new Germany. No small order. He could easily have caved in and allowed these titanic decisions to align themselves with the spreading web of corruption - the culture of back-handers already defining post-war Germany. Indeed, it is often represented that the process was perfunctory, ineffective and absurd. *Perfunctory* it was certainly not – and I can demonstrate that. *Ineffective* is an accusation that raises more delicate matters. To be ineffective would mean good men and women unjustly denied a livelihood. Equally, it would leave evil men and women free to exert authority. Errors in both directions would have consequences for Oscar, albeit at a later date and on another stage. He must have known this and must have been filled with foreboding. As to whether the process was *absurd* (although the word is inappropriate), much depends on judgements about the kind of social action psychology can legitimately carry out. Psychologists continue to deliberate on that and we shall come back to the question. For the moment, I will set out exactly what Oscar did. It does not seem perfunctory to me.

The Assessment Centre at Bad Oeynhausen consisted of the Officer in charge, together with a psychiatrist, an administrative officer, two testing officers and four psychologists. Twelve individuals (known as "candidates") were dealt with each week, arriving on Monday afternoon and leaving on Friday morning. Friday afternoon was used to make a determination for each candidate. Reports, prepared on Saturday, determined whether a candidate would ever work in the German State and at what level. The recommendations could be brutal. For example, Oscar's final report on someone described by his fellow candidates as "rather jolly," read: "This man is highly dangerous and should not be employed at any level or in any circumstances."

The most succinct account of the process is in a report prepared by two visiting American majors. I have abbreviated it, but it is worth quoting in detail, because it illustrates how much the procedures adopted owed to the psychoanalytic orientation of Oscar's Dundee days of peer assessment and functional penetration.

It starts on Monday with all of the candidates filling out a highly detailed questionnaire, which dealt with their political background and the political activities of their parents and their nearest relatives. On Tuesday morning, each candidate was asked to provide a five-minute oral resume of his background and professional life. Everyone, including all of the staff, was present. Three tests followed: the first part was a nonverbal intelligence test using visual pattern completion problems. The second part dealt with reasoning. The third was both a written and an oral word association test. The fifth and final test of the morning was a self-description by the candidate, first as his best friend would see him, and then as a strong critic would see him. After Tuesday's lunch candidates were divided into two groups. The first group began with individual assessment: a political interview of about one and half hours and a psychiatric interview of about one and half hours. The president and the psychiatrist interviewed four candidates each on Tuesday, Wednesday, and Thursday. While the first group was being individually studied, the second group had further group tests. The first was a group discussion over a 90 minute time period. The groups were asked to spend approximately 30 minutes discussing each of three topics: personal happiness, relationship of family and state, and Germany's contribution to European reconstruction. After this, each candidate gave a talk without preparation lasting for five minutes on special assignments, for example "a school superintendent addresses his teachers on corporal punishment, a chief of police addresses policemen on black market activities.

A sociological questionnaire followed, eliciting information about a candidate's fundamental political trends and social outlook. Each of the candidates then interviewed another for approximately 20 minutes in the presence of the staff, obtaining information on personal interests, hobbies, and recreational activities. There followed the "protest test." Candidates imagined themselves in a difficult situation and defended their position in the face of stern, unsympathetic criticism and frustrating behavior on the part of the examiners. This was followed by a "group-planning test," the groups asked to formulate a solution to a problem in county administration based upon letters, statistics, and a map of the county concerned. Then a team negotiation test, in which one of the groups was asked to represent a local German government committee and the other to represent the British military government detachment. They were to work out a solution to a problem, presented in the form of legal briefs.

Following all this, the entire group undertook a mutual evaluation. Candidates rating one another in terms of: leadership qualities, reliability, and friendship worthiness. The candidates left the center on Friday morning.

The modern Germany in large measure grew out of this process, along with a similar one in the American zone. What Oscar devised is as interesting for the techniques left out as for those actually employed. You can find no attempt to measure eidetic imagery; no sensory perceptual measurement; no reaction time. In fact no laboratory tasks at all apart from word association – a procedure that owes more to Jung than to Bartlett. All this devised by a psychologist who, not long before, had been completely immersed in laboratory measurement. The assessment process at Bad Oeynhausen owed vastly more to Dundee than to either Marburg or Cambridge.

CHAPTER 11

A reckoning

By the time I arrived in Melbourne in the 1960s, Oscar had been The Prof for almost twenty years. He was the first professor of psychology in the university and the department he created was unlike any other in Australia. I hasten to add, this was not necessarily a Good Thing.

His own arrival must have been bewildering. He had travelled in relative, and well-deserved, luxury, but there were others who had not. Among the influx of European refugees seeking a new life in Australia were many ex-Nazis. Jewish families would arrive on the dockside in Melbourne bitterly complaining they had been forced to share their journey with the very guards who had tormented them in death camps. The ambiguity of the word "sanctuary" haunts Australian politics to this day, because, for its own reasons, the Lucky Country extended a welcome to the very people Oscar, in his Bad Oeynhausen days, might have described as "extremely dangerous." He must have known at the time this was a possibility, and dreaded it. Post-war Australia was not uniquely culpable in this shameful business; both Britain and the United States also weighed the scientific or political value of particular individuals against their previous misdeeds, sometimes quite horrendous misdeeds. But the "whites only" immigration policy in Australia at that time made the hurt particularly acute. Remembering Marburg, what would Oscar have made of solemn deliberations on the whiteness of Jews? He surely resented the fact this undeclared Nazi invasion could mean a lifetime looking over his shoulder; a lifetime taking care going home at night. And what was he expected to make of the fact that people swilling about in the criminal underbelly of Melbourne knew more of the activities of Wing Commander Oeser than his own colleagues would ever know?

In hindsight, even in that initial encounter, terrifying though I found it, Oscar was a sad character, secretive and isolated. As I grew to know him better he seemed almost to be living in the wrong century – someone with an encyclopaedic knowledge of psychology wilfully divorced from the current preoccupations of the discipline. By which I mean, of course, my own preoccupations: the preoccupations of the humble galley slave. It didn't take me long to work out that Oscar wanted to change the world. Had I not been so frightened of him I would have explained that my generation generally settled for less than that. And all those big questions that had tempted him away from physics? I would have explained we'd given up on those, long before.

The fact was, psychology in the 1960s, had determined to concern itself with almost any animal but man. Behaviourism ruled. Clark Hull and Kenneth Spence set the agenda (and if you want to know the force of fashion, ask who now knows these faded titans?). Motivation was still centre stage, but defined solely, and with a perfectly straight face, in terms of the basic drives of rats. If the object of study was to be behaviour then, it was argued, rats were the organism of choice. Or possibly pigeons: sometimes people moved up to pigeons. Because, plainly, both rats and pigeons behave. They are also cheap to feed, ask for little in their humdrum lives, and don't answer back. Indeed, they can't speak at all – something counted as a decided blessing. They can, however, run or peck (as the case may be) and are capable of learning. These small animals provided behaviour in the raw – all you needed to establish general laws. Psychology at that time was awfully keen on Laws. How we yearned to have something like Boyle's Law or Ohm's Law to brandish in front of the doubters. You see, we had embraced a new Great Project: isolating the basic laws of behaviour using animal models. Once again, the study of mind was postponed. We would ascend to the human condition by extrapolation, as it were, at some later date. Don't laugh - we really did believe that.

Oscar looked on and wept. He thought it ridiculous nonsense. In 1957, in the foreword to a book, he wrote:

> *When, about the middle of the nineteenth century, the science of experimental psychology was born, the infant was crippled by an array of physical and physiological instruments. It was starved on a diet of psychophysics and later of rats. Put less metaphorically, for close on a century psychologists refused to regard the person as an appropriate unit on which to focus their studies. Only the psychoanalytic schools tried to understand the person.*

There is more than a dash of bitterness here. Plainly he was thinking of Jaensch and Bartlett. Perhaps a little disingenuously, because he had been committed enough at the time. Perhaps he was thinking about all those lost days, all those lost hopes. The pity was, none of us even knew about his Marburg or Cambridge days, lost or otherwise. And we knew nothing of Bletchley Park – how could we have known – it was a secret. We had not the faintest idea what Oscar had been up to in Bad Oeynhausen, or in Dundee for that matter. We had no idea that he actually had good reasons to believe a psychology of the person was possible; that psychology could address acute social problems; even solve them. He just seemed to be an old chap sidelined by the march of history. We didn't know – and he couldn't tell us.

The Melbourne curriculum was demanding. Oscar believed students should understand the basis of personality; grapple with the cause of mental disintegration; examine the dynamics of group behaviour; analyse peculiarly human concerns and try to understand. He thought it was beyond absurd to imagine that that understanding could be found in the study of starvation and copulation in rats. Alas, nobody was listening, including most of the psychologists in his Melbourne department. Including me, I regret to say. Here is perhaps the most shocking truth in science: *fashion matters*. Social psychology was out of fashion; clinical psychology, even more so; Freud was viewed in Melbourne with a suspicion even greater than in St Andrews; Jung's ideas (always close to Oscar's heart) were thought cranky and irrelevant. In a nutshell, the department Harry had sent me to - Oscar's department - was completely out of step with the fashionable concerns of the time.

I arrived to discover in The Prof an embattled man, apparently holding back the march of progress. It is too late now to say his critics were wrong; to say that we were wrong; to say that I was wrong. Science has its fashions, but it also has its martyrs. Oscar's error was to see himself as above the fray. Made necessarily remote by his secret past, he allowed himself to drift into a state of chronic unpopularity. He had inured himself to a role as the man in the wrong – perhaps he rather liked it. He must have felt frustrated, nonetheless – forced by his secret past into an apparently unjustified righteousness. He knew more than we did, on almost every level, but he had no way of conveying this. And then there was that fatal flaw - just as in St Andrews, if offence was taken, his instinctive response was to redouble the offence.

I can explain at last why thinking about my dad reminded me of this scary man with his extraordinary catalogue of secret achievements. It suggests something quite baffling about how memory works. Whatever it is we fish out of that deep well, it is surely not the facts of the matter. A moment's reflection and you realise how fragmentary is our record of events, how incomplete everything is, how unlike our world is from that of others. We cherish the wholeness of our memory and worry when gaps appear, but in truth it is full of gaps. Facts, such as they are, are just the crumbs. Huge organising themes continually circle above them, ready to swoop on the scraps we have discovered or fabricated, transforming them to something else; organising themes with the potency of fictional plots. My dad's story has elements in common with Oscar's story – elements that have motivated countless works of literature. You can put it into clumsy words if you like: how about *shame for virtue appreciated too late?* There's a plot that served Homer as well as Dickens. Bartlett called such abstract themes *schema*; it's a vague term, although in truth nobody has come up with anything much better and we don't know much more about the process now than we did in Bartlett's day. Being deprived of that spot in the car park made me remember the slice of fish because the same organising theme alighted on the facts of the matter. You could call that story *selfish dispossession* if you like, the name doesn't matter: what does matter is that I will, in my lifetime, deploy it thousands of times and it will help stitch together the web of things I call my mental life.

It is worth asking what organising themes motivated Oscar's inner story. And my dad's, come to that. How did they deal with the fact that those around them would never know their worth, or know it too late? *The Scarlet Pimpernel* re-written – his wife and friends never discover his virtuous secret. *Great Expectations* re-written – Pip clings onto his delusion. Suddenly things take a rather sour turn. My dad never explained his suicidal occupation: perhaps he lived (and died) believing he was owed something. It was not good for him, this secret knowledge. As the years passed he grew more short-tempered, even a little tyrannical. And Oscar? The perceived slight was greater, written on a vastly wider canvas. Truly, he had cause to expect, if not veneration, a kind of respect. Anonymous donors are told their reward is in heaven: God knows their secret. It may not be enough. There is not much consolation in a hair shirt. As the years passed, Oscar grew less inclined to argue his corner, less tolerant, a little tyrannical. Finally, he was disenchanted. At a number of critical points in his life, psychology had cast its spell. In the end, the enchantment had gone; and if I have written this for no other reason it is to explain, too late, that I do not grudge him the sentiment.

Oscar knew he was not much liked. He had read his Jung, so I assume he understood why; indeed, he surely understood better than me, although perhaps his conclusions were not so very different from mine. How would someone soured by knowledge respond to a situation he could neither mend nor reverse? At least one response was characteristic of the man. You recall his asking me once about a picture? It is there in the background of my treasured group photograph. Fixed rather incongruously to the famously dusty brickwork of the Redmond Barry Building. Given it was a gift, and given he was not anybody's favourite uncle right then, we would have been wise to reflect on other stories about unwonted gifts. The painting was by Paul Nash, entitled *Vernal Equinox III*. Nash finished it at the war's end, in 1944, a significant date for Oscar. It shows a wooded knoll, possibly a prehistoric burial mound, and a surrounding landscape in bleached colours. There are no figures - humanity is missing altogether - but the sun and the moon are both visible in a quiet sky filled with bars of cloud. Nash painted several landscapes like this. All have the same melancholy nostalgic feel about them, redolent of an old England, forever lost. Living in Melbourne - about as far as you can from England – it is an ironic choice, with its understated patriotic qualities. This, as the journalists were wont to say, is what we were all fighting for. If so, the painting suggests little pleasure in the prize, just an air of nostalgic melancholy, a sense of things gone for good. Jung had written about the vernal equinox at about the time Oscar made the presentation:

> *Considering the terrible time in which we are living, it reminds me of those dark centuries when the culture of antiquity was gradually falling into decay. Now once again we are in a time of decay and transition. The vernal equinox is moving out of the sign of Pisces into the sign of Aquarius. Our apocalyptic epoch contains the seeds of a different, unprecedented, and still inconceivable future. The coming new age will be as vastly*

different from ours as the world of the 19th century was from that of the 20th with its atomic physics and its psychology of the unconscious. Never before has mankind been torn into two halves, and never before was the power of absolute destruction given into the hand of man himself. It is a "godlike" power that has fallen into human hands.

How quickly we seem to have forgotten the apocalyptic pessimism of those times, when we breathed in fear along with the nuclear fallout. It must have been far worse for those, like Oscar, who believed they had secured just deliverance from a terrible conflict. For those with a "good war" behind them, to use that sneering phrase, imminent nuclear extinction must have seemed like a God's last sick joke. I'm sure Oscar at that time was a deeply disillusioned man. Nonetheless, he could not resist making the gift into a complicated joke at his own expense. It was a joke from a man who had devoted his war to decoding fish, about the end of the age of fish. Farewell to all that. Not that anybody knew at the time, or could possibly have known; secrets and all that.

Incidentally, Oscar had been born a fish (on February 22nd). However, unlike the hippies, he clearly viewed the dawning of the Age of Aquarius with distaste. We may assume he mourned the end of the age - the end of his age; indeed, the end of a faith which, to paraphrase Jung, was built on fish. Little wonder Oscar was in the habit of asking people what they made of the picture - I can see him enjoying the joke. As you know, he asked me, and I know now what I might have said. But I am fifty years too late.

I was working on my novel *Lucy* when I set it aside to let this search for Oscar take over my life. His biography intersected with my autobiography because our lives crossed. He was a quite extraordinary man who did quite extraordinary things. A man who kept quiet and suffered for his silence. A man who knew and worked alongside many of the characters who shaped the last century, for good or ill. He did heroic things. He was extraordinarily well-informed. He practised psychology for nearly sixty years. Yet nobody has heard of him. For different unjustified reasons, Marburg, Cambridge, St Andrews, Dundee, Melbourne – all of them – have either rubbed his name out of the book or left him as a perfunctory footnote.

When I finally returned to my novel it was almost a surprise to discover how much thoughts of Oscar were weaving themselves into the text. His name, of course. But beyond that, Dundee – a place imposing itself against my best intentions. I had thought to set the book in Edinburgh, but Oscar's Dundee took its place: a city haunted by its grim past, a hard place to live in, yet somewhere which, however indirectly, helped shape our modern world. Originally, I intended my character's name as no more than a whimsical nod to my long-dead mentor. But although I was eager to pin him down, the character that emerged preferred the shadows. He resisted all efforts to know him.

If you were looking for an epitaph for Oscar, that might serve.

Acknowledgements

Particular thanks to my wife Elizabeth who took the cover photograph and made innumerable suggestions which have improved the text. Graham Lane, Alan Wilkes and Trevor Harley commented on the final version. What remains is my responsibility alone.

Also by Alan Kennedy

The Boat in the Bay [ISBN 978-0-9564696-0-1]

Initially, this might be the story Arthur Ransome never got round to writing. But these children do not lead a charmed life. They are given to making mistakes. Their anxieties and fears are more pressing and, although they do their best, their world is not always kind. They must learn that things do not invariably turn out well. Minor mishaps that might happen to anybody slowly become threatening. Trivial decisions have distant and dreadful consequences. Problems that appear solved turn out to be anything but and become the seeds of something altogether out of control. In a terrifying climax, the children eventually discover the secret of the old boat moored in the bay, but at an awful cost. When courage and resourcefulness are spent, there is only luck to draw on, and it is uncertain who will survive.

The Broken Bell [ISBN 978-0-9564696-3-2]

This is the sequel to *The Boat in the Bay*. It features the same characters in new surroundings. When Uncle Albert arranges a surprise holiday for the children, he imagines he's looking after them, after his own fashion. But things don't always turn out quite the way you expect and before the story ends it is he in need of help. In desperate need, in fact, with his life hanging on a thread and only the children to save him in a frantic race against time. The story leads to a dramatic climax on a remote island in unfriendly seas, cut off from the familiar world. And we learn how an idyllic holiday can go badly wrong. *The Broken Bell* is a book about the acute pains of coming to terms with foreign places and foreign ways. It also gives a first glimpse of Poppy as a painter, hardly aware of her own prodigious talent. The hero, however, is the youngest of them all. Ian never completely understands what is going on, but he saves the day, nonetheless.

The Pink House [ISBN 978-0-9564696-4-9]

This sequel to *The Broken Bell* finds the children growing apart. Poppy must chose between painting and adventure as the others discover a lost lake in a secret valley. The decision to stay behind and begin her first painting changes her life for ever as, too late, she discovers the dreadful consequence of their discovery. Set between the wars, the action is seen through the eyes of children confronting a world they never quite understand. At one level an adventure story, at another, a spellbinding account of a child's first steps in the dark world of art and artists. A book about love and loss and the power of art.

Lucy [ISBN 978-0-9564696-7-0]

Twenty years have passed. Poppy is a successful painter, dividing her life between London and France. She has fame, money and reputation. She also has Oscar. At least, he has always been there. One fine day, she will do something about that. It was, as she says herself, hardly a love affair, more a kind of marriage. But she is deceiving herself – something she discovers at dreadful cost when she finds herself trapped in wartime Vichy France. Set before and after WWII in London, Edinburgh, Saint-Valery-sur-Somme, Dundee, and a remote village in war-time France: two painters struggle to come to terms with the casual brutality of war.

www.ingramcontent.com/pod-product-compliance
Lightning Source LLC
Chambersburg PA
CBHW051710040426
42446CB00008B/817